PRAISE

I'm Such a Messterpiece is a must-read! Andrea keeps it raw and real as she takes us through the real-life issues of mental health, anxiety, and panic attacks—things that aren't talked about enough in the church. Her beautiful story of redemption points us to hope, encourages us to be honest about our struggles, and reminds us that Jesus loves us no matter what.

—Ashley Henriott
TikTok mom, coach, and podcast host of *Confidence and Coffee*

Andrea Nyberg skillfully draws her reader into her story of a life that is hard and sometimes messy. Like a warm blanket for those caught in the cold reality of their own mess, Andrea's words bring hope. As someone who has struggled with the shame of depression as a Christian, I think this book is invaluable.

—Debbie Alsdorf
Author of *It's Momplicated, Deeper,* and *The Faith Dare*

Dealing with mental struggles in a Christian context has often been restrictive and can be more weighty than helpful. Andrea graciously invites the reader into her struggles with anxiety and depression as well as everyday mental battles in a way that breaks down the isolating shame these feelings bring. Then she gives many tools, along with reminders of godly truths, to help silence the lies. Read this book as fast or slow as you'd like, but be sure to reflectively work through the applications.

—Drew Froese
Lead pastor of Real Life Christian Church in North Chesapeake, VA
Author of *Faith Full: A Practical Guide For FULLY Living Out Your Faith*

The church has long encouraged the integration of our emotional and physical health, even in the midst of sickness and suffering, alongside our spiritual health as a means for flourishing. However, we've not often taken this same view of mental health. In fact, we've often pushed mental health to the side or largely ignored it. That is why *I'm Such a Messterpiece* is a welcome book, because it walks us through how to integrate our mental health alongside our emotional, physical, and spiritual health so that we can flourish as followers of Jesus without having to leave any part of us behind or neglected. I believe Andrea's offering will serve the church well for years to come!

—Chris Wilson
Lead pastor/planter of Restoration Church in Wilmington, NC

i'M SUCH A

MESSTERPiECE.

ANDREA M. NYBERG

I'M SUCH A MESSTERPIECE

Shattering Stigmas, (Re)Framing Our Fears,
and Finding Ourselves Fully Loved

REDEMPTION PRESS

Published by Redemption Press, PO Box 427, Enumclaw, WA 98022.
Toll-Free (844) 2REDEEM (273-3336)

Redemption Press is honored to present this title in partnership with the author. The views expressed or implied in this work are those of the author. Redemption Press provides our imprint seal representing design excellence, creative content, and high-quality production.

The author has tried to recreate events, locales, and conversations from memories of them. In order to maintain their anonymity, in some instances the names of individuals, some identifying characteristics, and some details may have been changed, such as physical properties, occupations, and places of residence.

ISBN 13: 978-1-64645-494-5 (Paperback)
978-1-951310-81-3 (Audiobook)
978-1-64645-492-1 (ePub)

Library of Congress Catalog Card Number: 2022923589

DEDICATION

To every person who has felt the weight of loving Jesus while living with mental, emotional, and physical illness.

Acknowledgments

A book is a story held together by its characters. Main roles, supporting roles, and surprise roles develop the dynamic and fill the chapters with suspense, love, heartbreak, and triumph. My life, and yours, is like a book filled with people who have shaped our stories. To give each person in my story a proper acknowledgment would require a book of its own. But I would like to recognize the lead characters during this chapter of my life who helped bring the book you are holding into the world.

To my Sovereign Lord, thank you for never letting me go. Thank you for sending the help I needed—through friends, family, therapists, education, and medication—so I could once again see clearly who I am and whose I am. Thank you for showing me the masterpiece within the mess. Thank you for teaching me how to reframe my perspective in order to reclaim my hope in you and for using my story to bring hope and solidarity to others. May it be so.

To Eric, my husband and best friend, your faithfulness has held our family together. Thank you for riding these illogical, unpredictable, fierce waves with me. Thank you for carrying the burden of chronic illness with me. Thank you for being my partner through it all. I love you forever.

To Chloe and Eliott, my precious children, you have shaped and sharpened me to seek Jesus every day. In spite of how often I'll miss the mark, I pray your story is shaped by knowing God's never-ending, unchanging love for you as His children. He is faithful and trustworthy. Remain in His love, my darlings. He will always help you, strengthen you, and hold you up.

To Stephanie, my sister, thank you for always being my biggest fan and cheerleader.

To Joy, my mother-in-love, I'll never forget our chat at the beach house in the summer of 2014. Thank you for assuring me that I would never be alone on this journey.

To Shelby Hall, thank you for inviting me to your youth group in eighth grade. My life changed forever that night.

To Rebekah Laffoon, thank you for taking a minute out of your day to offer support and resources in response to my Facebook post. It was a life raft that kept me from drowning.

To all my MOPS mamas, you welcomed me, listened to me, made space for me, taught me, invested in me, and then buoyed me up as a leader. I would not be who I am today were it not for you. A special shoutout to my GLAD gathering gals: Amanda Froese, Amanda Studer, Kimberly Hock, Krystal Griffiths, Naiomi Evans, Olivia Tessmer, Terri Rutledge, and Vanessa Floyd. You helped me break down the walls of my insecurities and showed me what true friendship looks like.

To my therapist, Janie Sacks, your gentle nudges toward truth changed the trajectory of my life and invited me into a new narrative. Thank you.

To my Life Skills leaders, Diane and Meghann, thank you for volunteering your time to lead a group of hurting women into hope and healing.

To Ann Kroeker and the Spring 2020 Craft a Compelling Book Proposal group, what a gift to lay the foundations of our books together.

To Anita Tighe and Julie Landreth, thank you for being my prayer warriors. Knowing I had you in my corner kept me strong through the battle of bringing these words into the world.

To my early readers, Amanda Studer, Amanda Lewallen, Carey Hall Waldrop, and Jolene Hall, thank you for your time and thoughtful feedback. It was invaluable.

To Frances Tuck, thank you for pointing me back to "the last thing God asked me to do" and for being a steady voice of reason and reflection when I got stuck.

To Krystal, Amanda, Eric, Stephanie, and Frankie, thank you for enduring my million front cover mockups. Y'all are the best!

To Jennifer Edwards, my writing coach and editor, you made me a better writer from day one.

To Athena Dean Holtz, Dori Harrell, Becky Antkowiak, Jennifer Fedler, and the team at Redemption Press, thank you for your support and partnership in bringing this project to life.

Disclaimer

This book is not a replacement for therapy or medical care. I am not a doctor, therapist, or scientist. If you are not yet under the care of a doctor or therapist, know that there is no shame in getting the medical and professional help you need. Your life matters, and it is worth investing in.

If you are feeling suicidal, there is 24/7 support available to you. You can call the National Suicide Prevention Lifeline at 988 (the new three-digit dialing code), chat with a support staff member at https://988lifeline.org/chat/, or text HOME to 741741 to reach the Crisis Text Line and connect with a trained crisis counselor.

This book is also not a replacement for Scripture. We will look at Bible passages in each chapter, but the main goal is for you to know you're not alone in your questions, doubts, and fears. Keep going back to God's Word, opening your Bible, and looking to Him for the truth, wisdom, and peace only He can provide.

Our shared experience is a holy gift. God gave us community, and we're in this together. But apart from Him, we can do nothing (John 15:5). Only God can do the true work of transformation.

CONTENTS

START HERE!
YOU ARE NOT ALONE

HAVE YOU EVER FELT LIKE a prisoner in your own body—gripped by fear and hopelessness while holding everything you ever prayed for? Do you struggle with feeling like too much and not enough—convinced you are unwelcome, unwanted, and unable to overcome the pain of your past? Have you turned to God's Word for comfort only to feel like a failure because you have mustered up every ounce of faith within you, but the mountains just won't move?

Me too, friend. Me too.

We may not know each other personally, but I want you to know I don't take the word *friend* lightly. If we're not friends yet, I pray we will be by the end of our journey together through this book. And as your friend, I just want to say I'm sorry. I'm sorry for the pain you're holding. I'm sorry for the times you've reached out for help and love and were scolded and misunderstood. I'm sorry for the confusion you've felt in your relationship with God as you try to figure out how to love Jesus while living with anxiety, depression, insecurity, and self-sabotage.

And let me assure you of this—you are not alone.

Perhaps, like me, you have suppressed your instinct to seek medical or professional help because you're convinced this is a lack of faith on your part. When I hit rock bottom, I was desperate for resources to help me understand what was happening and how to cope. The first book I read on faith and mental health promised to point me toward hope but left me feeling more ashamed and alone than ever. The author espoused the belief that anxiety and depression were not diseases that could effectively be treated with medication but rather symptoms of a deeper issue that could only be healed through hope in Christ.

Now here's where I want to be very clear. The hope of Christ is what offers us the deepest healing and the truest freedom. The triune God is all-sufficient to meet our needs. The problem is anxiety, depression, and shame can blind us to the truth and freedom available to us in Christ. Having personally experienced this and talked to countless others with similar stories, I firmly believe these conditions can manifest as diseases that require medical intervention for some. The number of cases of anxiety and depression reported each year, along with the millions of prescriptions filled, is astounding, and this epidemic begs for further study. There is no question that deeper work is required to get to the root of these debilitating issues. And while popping a pill won't magically solve our problems, medication can offer the relief and healthy frame of mind needed to do the deeper soul work ahead. For many of us, it's *both/and*.

We'll dive deep into this conversation in chapter 6, but for now, please hear this: if you're struggling with anxiety, depression, or any other invisible disease, don't feel ashamed to seek medical and professional help. Therapy is a gift. Every single human alive can benefit from it. And medication may or may not be the right fit for you, but there is no shame in weighing it as an option. Medication does not replace your faith in God. It is simply one tool of many to help clear the fog of fear and sadness so you can more fully experience God's love for you. If you're anything like me and long for the support of others, consider this a bona fide stamp of approval to get the care you need.

You are not the first, nor will you be the last, to have this depleting familiarity with the battle of faith and mental illness and all the stigmas that come along with it.

You're not crazy.

You're not imagining things.

It's not all in your head.

And it's not a sole matter of faith.

The Messterpiece

For many of us, the roots of our pain stem from unhealed childhood traumas that have stunted our ability to flourish emotionally, mentally, physically, and spiritually. From this space, shame has caused us to believe we're bad, broken, and hopeless, and fear has robbed us of peace and joy. But there's still good news to be held in this hard space. No matter how bad, broken, or hopeless we feel, nothing can change the fact that we are God's magnum opus—His greatest work as an artist. We were made in His image (Genesis 1:26–28) and crafted by His holy hands (Psalm 139)—and that makes us a masterpiece (Ephesians 2:10).

The pain of this season is real. The hope of this season is equally real. Life is not without suffering, but suffering is not without hope. It's both/and. And so are we. We are simultaneously living in the mess while living as the masterpiece of God—a paradox I affectionately call a *messterpiece*. A messterpiece represents the collision of pain and hope, joy and sorrow, the now and the not yet. It's an invitation to (re)frame our circumstances through the lens of God's faithfulness and unending love for us. Let me tell you how (re)framing began for me.

The Roots of (Re)framing

Two years into our marriage, my husband and I began dreaming about starting a family. Naturally, the first thing we did to prepare for such a big decision was book a ten-day trip to Europe. We needed to get a few stamps on our passports before venturing into the foreign land of parenthood. In preparation for our trip, my husband surprised me with a gift. Oh boy, do I love surprises! The package was large and heavy, and joyful anticipation ran hot through my fingers as I held the box. With a final rip of the wrapping paper, I squealed with excitement to see an entry-level, professional camera. Wow!

Unbeknownst to me, my husband had taken notice of my resolve to document the world around me, and he wanted me to have a worthy tool to capture the streets of Italy and the history of France. It was a sleek and sturdy machine that fit just right in my hands. As I poked my way around the settings and peered through the lens, I saw flashbacks of family get-togethers, talent shows, vacations, and simple Tuesdays. And there I was, camera in hand, eager to capture the moments that would all too soon become memories. What I had long overlooked came into clear focus . . . I was a photographer.

What began as a means to document our pre-parenthood pleasure cruise became a tool that launched my professional photography career. While newer, fancier models have replaced my starter kit, I'll never forget the joy and fascination of receiving my first real camera. Through that lens, I learned to see myself and the world around me in a new way. Through that lens, God showed me how to (re)frame.

Reframe. REframe. reFRAME. (RE)frame.

However you write it, (re)framing is an invitation to shift our perspective and examine what we see, think, feel, and believe from a different angle. Sometimes we need the onlooking eye of someone who loves us to show us what we can't yet see. And no one else knows us better or loves us more than our Creator God. I'm challenged daily to consider the lens I'm looking through and evaluate if there's another angle waiting for me, should I choose to see it. I invite you to do the same.

The learning curve on mastering a camera's manual mode is steep, but the learning curve on life, marriage, and motherhood is much steeper. Unlike a camera, life has no manual for how to get the precise outcome we desire. The Giver of Life, on the other hand, provides us with a tool much more powerful than any step-by-step instruction guide. He offers Himself. His wisdom. His understanding. His perspective. God's Word gives us everything we need to live a life filled with joy, wonder, and purpose. It also gives us what we need when life is not so joyful, wonderful, or rich with resolve. Sometimes we can't see what's right in front of us because things are out of focus or smudged. And anxiety and depression certainly have a knack for making it hard to grasp the truth of Scripture, don't they?

The Power of Perspective

One of the greatest goals of this book is to change the lens of our faith, identity, and mental health from an either/or to a both/and perspective.

To move from the shame of questioning, "How can I be a Christian who struggles with anxiety and depression?" to the freedom of being curious about, "How can I learn to embrace God's love for me and learn to love myself in the midst of my anxiety, depression, doubt, and fear?" Making this paradigm shift will require getting to the root of what we believe and why we believe it, and this begins with asking good questions.

My therapist, Janie, is a master question-asker. There were a few noteworthy instances during my time in therapy when I was in the middle of a major breakdown, and Janie would ask me a question that (re)framed everything and started me on a new path. You'll encounter her insightful wisdom throughout the pages of this book.

Additionally, one of the most helpful tools I've found is the Belief Tree.[1] Darlene Cunningham, founder of YWAM (Youth with a Mission), found inspiration from Donald Miller's tree diagram when crafting her own version. Miller suggests that what we believe—our roots—is linked to how we behave—our fruit.[2] Cunningham takes it a step further by asking us to consider whether our beliefs, values, and behaviors reflect the truth of Jesus.[3] I've put a photographer's spin on Cunningham's five-stage progression and will refer to it as The (Re)framing Process.

At the end of each chapter, we will use this as a guide to help get to the root of what we believe and why we believe it. Only then can we assess the areas that need to be (re)framed so we can step into deeper healing and fuller freedom.

THE (RE)FRAMING PROCESS

CAMERA = WORLDVIEW (WHAT IS REAL?)

LENS = BELIEFS (WHAT IS TRUE?)

VIEWFINDER = VALUES (WHAT IS GOOD?)

CLICK = CHOICES (WHAT IS RIGHT?)

DISPLAY = RESULT (WHAT IS WISE?)

CAMERA = SOIL/WORLDVIEW (What is real?)

In preparation for a photo session, the first thing I do is choose and prepare the camera I plan to use. I charge the battery and clear old photos from the memory cards. The body of the camera represents our worldview—initially founded in the viewpoints and positions of our caregivers.

LENS = ROOTS/BELIEFS (What is true?)

Once the body of the camera is set up, I choose the best lens for the type of session I'm photographing. Once I make my choice, I use a soft cloth to carefully remove any dirt or smudges from the glass. I then attach the lens to the body of the camera and set them into my camera bag. The lens represents the roots where our beliefs are formed—an instrument to examine what is true. What we believe to be true about ourselves, others, and God will either lead us to hope or heartache.

VIEWFINDER = TRUNK/VALUES (What is good?)

When I arrive on site for the photo session, I lift my camera out of the bag, swing the strap around my neck, remove the lens cover, then press my eye against the viewfinder to assess the scene around me. I search for the good spots where shimmers of sunlight play peek-a-boo from behind golden leaves, creating a glorious glow behind bouncy curls or sharp suits. Like the trunk of the tree, my viewfinder verifies what I value—what I believe to be good.

What we believe will become what we value. If we believe we are valuable, we will pursue things that honor our unique design. If we believe we are worthless, we will discount our merit and sit stuck on the bench of "could've, should've, would've," feeling hopelessly flawed.

CLICK = BRANCHES/CHOICES (What is right?)

To ensure the goodness in front of me is captured in clear focus, I check my settings next. Is my shutter speed high enough? Is my aperture set at the correct exposure for the number of people in the shot? Is auto focus working well, or do I need to switch to manual mode? Few things are more frustrating to a photographer than a blurry face in a photo—especially when I have the tools and knowledge to get a stunning image if I set my camera up correctly. The only way to truly know if the image will flop or fly is to take a test shot. I press down halfway on the shutter release button, listen for the cue that it's in focus, and click! The decisions that lead up to the act of taking the photo are like the branches of the tree—the limbs we go out on, if you will. Here we decide what is right.

We will eventually begin to make decisions for ourselves based on the foundations of our worldview, beliefs, and values. Here, we start to practice what we know, or think we know, and search for what we don't know, or think we don't know.

DISPLAY = FRUIT/RESULT (What is wise?)

In digital photography, the fruit of our labor is instantly displayed on a small LCD screen on the back of the camera. Within moments of taking the test shot, we can assess if we made wise choices throughout the process and if we are satisfied with the final result. The good news is, if the image wasn't what we were hoping for, we can make adjustments. While the fruit of our life choices is not always instantly reviewable, we can still make modifications to achieve a different end result—just like on a camera. We can learn to create a legacy rather than cause a landslide by correcting our settings, moving into more light, and changing the lens when needed.

Where the Spirit of the Lord Is, There Is Freedom

The ultimate purpose of (re)framing is to find freedom in our faith, identity, and mental health. I had never grasped that freedom more deeply than in the 2017/2018 season of MOPS (Mothers of Preschoolers). I know, strange name for a mom's group, right? But this group has been one of the greatest blessings of my adult life.

Each year, the team at MOPS International announces a theme that will guide the weekly gatherings of women across the globe. Our rally cry that year was "Free Indeed," and the task of our leadership team was to encourage our women to embrace the freedom Jesus proclaimed when He began His ministry: "The Spirit of the LORD is upon me, for he has anointed me to bring Good News to the poor. He has sent me to proclaim that captives will be released, that the blind will see, that the oppressed will be set free, and that the time of the LORD's favor has come" (Luke 4:18–19 NLT).

Fun fact: this was the official announcement to the people of Israel that the Messiah they had been waiting for had finally arrived. Jesus was fulfilling the prophecy from Isaiah 61 right before their eyes. Hope was here, and His name was Jesus.

As a MOPS group, we spent the year immersed in this passage, studying its context, considering its meaning, and contemplating its application to our lives today. And we all walked away better understanding that Jesus came to set the captives free! Not only free from an overbearing government but free from the weight of sin, shame, and fear. Free from legalism and lies. Free from hate and illness. Free from darkness. That is some seriously good news. It's actually the best news ever. And it's the roadmap that helped me build this book.

How to Use This Book

The principles in each chapter build upon each other, but the tools and prayers are designed to be easily referred back to. Each chapter ends with these three elements:

(Re)Frame It: Questions to help us identify how our beliefs affect our behavior, which lies need to be replaced with truth, and what steps we can take to move toward whole health.

Pray about It: An invitation to ask for God's help in (re)framing each belief, thought, feeling, and action through the lens of His love for us.

Messterpiece Reminder: A mantra from the theme of that chapter with a both/and focus.

My hope is that you will not only read the book but that you will grab a few friends and go through it together. The work we do in private is important and necessary. But true transformation happens in community.

I know how scary it is to open up, not knowing how people will react or what they'll think of you. That's why I'm going first. I'm putting all my cards on the table so you can feel the freedom to do the same. Every time we get real about our pain, stigmas weaken and hope rises. Each time we're honest, others feel free to be honest too. And that is where solidarity is found. It may not be pretty, but it has tremendous potential in helping us heal.

You're in the right place, friend. Christ told us we will suffer (John 16:33), but He also told us He's already overcome anything this world can throw at us. What you're facing right now is only a chapter in the story of your life. It is not the whole book. Not even close. So let's dive in. Let's begin the hard yet healing work of shattering stigmas, (re)framing our fears, and finding ourselves fully loved.

Let's unmask the masterpiece within the mess.

ISAIAH 61

The Year of the Lord's Favor

The Spirit of the Sovereign LORD is on me, because the LORD has anointed me to proclaim good news to the poor. He has sent me to bind up the brokenhearted, to proclaim freedom for the captives and release from darkness for the prisoners, to proclaim the year of the LORD's favor and the day of vengeance of our God, to comfort all who mourn, and provide for those who grieve in Zion—to bestow on them a crown of beauty instead of ashes, the oil of joy instead of mourning, and a garment of praise instead of a spirit of despair. They will be called oaks of righteousness, a planting of the LORD for the display of his splendor.

They will rebuild the ancient ruins and restore the places long devastated; they will renew the ruined cities that have been devastated for generations. Strangers will shepherd your flocks; foreigners will work your fields and vineyards. And you will be called priests of the LORD, you will be named ministers of our God. You will feed on the wealth of nations, and in their riches you will boast.

Instead of your shame you will receive a double portion, and instead of disgrace you will rejoice in your inheritance. And so you will inherit a double portion in your land, and everlasting joy will be yours.

"For I, the LORD, love justice; I hate robbery and wrongdoing. In my faithfulness I will reward my people and make an everlasting covenant with them. Their descendants will be known among the nations and their offspring among the peoples. All who see them will acknowledge that they are a people the LORD has blessed."

I delight greatly in the LORD; my soul rejoices in my God. For he has clothed me with garments of salvation and arrayed me in a robe of his righteousness, as a bridegroom adorns his head like a priest, and as a bride adorns herself with her jewels.

For as the soil makes the sprout come up and a garden causes seeds to grow, so the Sovereign LORD will make righteousness and praise spring up before all nations.

Chapter 1

CLEANING THE LENS OF MY FAITH

And you will be called priests of the Lord, you will be named ministers of
our God ... Instead of your shame you will receive a double portion, and
instead of disgrace you will rejoice in your inheritance ...
and everlasting joy will be yours.

Isaiah 61:6–7

YOU'D NEVER KNOW IT FROM my pale, freckled face and auburn hair, but I was born into a large, Italian-Greek family. My paternal grandfather was born just outside of Rome, and my maternal great-grandfather hailed from Greece. My mom is one of four, my dad is one of eight, and I have more cousins than I can count. We were never short on company or food.

Our family attended St. Paul Catholic Church in Whitehaven, Tennessee. The building was beautiful, and the atmosphere was thick with reverence. As we dipped our fingers in the holy water to anoint our heads before walking into the sanctuary, it was clear this was a sacred space. And something about that was comforting to me.

Beyond compare, the part I treasured most about Mass was the music. Voices lifted in heavenly harmony echoed off the stained-glass windows straight into the depths of my soul. Even at an early age, music overwhelmed me in the most mesmerizing way. It spoke to a space within me that nothing else could. The rest of the service blurred out as the choruses rang over and over in my head. This is probably why I never heard the message of the gospel clearly until I was much older.

"Being a Catholic is not what makes you a Christian," my grand-mother said to me once. I was around seven years old, and it would be years later before I fully grasped the meaning of her words.

Looking for Love

For various reasons, our family stopped attending church regularly for several years. But that changed for me in April 1996. It was my eighth-grade year, and there was this boy. His name was John, and I had drawn many hearts in my notebook with his name in it. At school one day, I overheard my friend, Shelby, mention something about a youth group on Wednesday night. Knowing she attended the same church as John, I casually strolled over to see what this was all about. "Do you want to come?" she eagerly invited. Why, yes. Yes, I would.

I thoughtfully considered what to wear and how to act so I was sure to catch his attention. This was the late nineties, so my boy-catcher bangs were armed and ready. Shelby and her dad picked me up, and we headed toward my destiny. I was sure this was the night he'd reciprocate his undying love for me. Okay, that may have been a tad far-reaching. But I wanted so much to catch his eye and to make an impression on his heart the way he had on mine.

I had never been to a youth group before, so I had no idea what to expect. Never in a million years was I expecting to begin the evening with a game where the pastor called for volunteers to put pantyhose over their heads and try to eat a banana. Was I at church or on an episode of *Double Dare*? It was great. After getting some sillies out, it was time to take a seat and hear a Bible lesson. I made sure we sat in clear eyeshot of John. But that was the last time I thought about him for the rest of the night.

As the pastor talked, I realized there was someone there who had an undying love for me. Someone whose eye I had caught. Someone I had made a lasting impression on. And His name was Jesus.

It's not that I had never heard about Jesus. I had just never heard His love explained so clearly. I grew up going to a priest to confess my sins. My understanding was that the priest talked to God on my behalf. I didn't realize I could talk to God directly because of what Jesus had done by dying and rising again. I didn't realize how much Jesus loved me. That He willingly died for me because He couldn't stand the thought of being separated from me. That He took on the penalty of all the things I had done and ever would do wrong to settle the score of sin and reconcile me to God the Father. What could compare to that kind of love?

When the official meeting ended, I ran up to talk to the pastor. I was an absolute blubbering mess. So overwhelmed with gratitude, I just kept thanking him for telling me about Jesus. I couldn't hold back my tears and fell into this poor pastor's arms—completely undone yet completely whole. On that Wednesday night in April 1996, I came to church with my friend Shelby to catch the eye of a boy. Instead, I caught the eye of Jesus, a man who captured my heart and never let go.

The Lens of Love

When we put our eyes up to the viewfinder of Scripture, we are invited to see things through the lens of God's unapologetic adoration for His creation. Through this lens of love, we can (re)frame everything we know because of who He is and who we are to Him.

As disciples of Jesus Christ, the Bible becomes the ultimate lens through which we frame our lives. The very words of God become the framework of our thoughts, decisions, beliefs, and behaviors. They are our source of hope, peace, and wisdom.

> All Scripture is inspired by God and is useful to teach us what is true and to make us realize what is wrong in our lives. It corrects us when we are wrong and teaches us to do what is right. God uses it to prepare and equip his people to do every good work. (2 Timothy 3:16–17 NLT)

But our faith in God tends to get pulled under the microscope when we experience pain. When our brains get hijacked by fear, our ability to rest in the truth of Scripture feels elusive. Even when we know deep down in our bones that we have been saved by His blood and washed as white as snow, the hope we have in Christ can be hard to hold on to when battling disorders of the mind.

Doubt became crippling for me as I wrestled with the validity of my faith in the midst of anxiety and depression. When I tried to read my Bible, the words of God—meant to offer help, hope, and healing—left me feeling more helpless, hopeless, and further hurt. All I could see was the face of a disappointed Father wagging His finger in my face telling me to stop worrying so much. I was trying not to be afraid, but fear had hijacked my brain. My fight-or-flight button was broken and stuck on overdrive.

"Don't be afraid" felt like salt on an open wound since I felt afraid of everything. "Ask and it will be given to you" cut deep, reminding me of the countless prayers that remained unanswered. All you need is "faith the size of a mustard seed and you can tell the mountain to move, and it will move" woke me to the reality that the only things moving were the swirling thoughts that had taken over my mind, making me feel like a broken and unrepairable mess.

What gives, God?

Perhaps you've experienced this distressing reality too?

I see now what I couldn't see during that debilitating season of anxiety and depression—God's command "do not be afraid" has much more to do with His faithfulness than with my faith. Through the lens of fear, it's all up to me and how much faith I can muster up. But in reality, it's all about Him and His faithfulness—no matter my circumstance.

God invites us again and again not to fear or be afraid because He never wants us to forget that we can trust Him. He will love us and be with us no matter how big of a mess we find ourselves in. I can't tell you how much that comforts me, because one of my biggest fears is being left behind or rejected because someone I love thinks I'm too much or not enough.

The truth is, some people will shun us, shame us, and leave us behind because they simply do not understand our struggle. When we reach out for support for anxiety and depression, they may tell us we just need to pray more, read our Bibles, and have more faith because they think that's the right answer to our problem. And the truth is, as a follower of Christ, we do need to pray, have faith, and saturate our minds with the truths of Scripture. But shame has never been the path to salvation. Only love.

Stories from Scripture

Jesus did not humiliate or dismiss people for their struggles. Quite the opposite. Throughout the Gospels, Jesus sought out and invited the most hated, the most unclean, and the most haunted to follow Him.

Jesus's mission was not to cast judgment on the people of this world but rather to eternally reconcile them to God the Father (John 12:44–50). As Jesus carries out His mission to save the world, we watch hopelessness turn to hope, disease turn to praise, and despair turn to joy again and again and again. All because of Him. Because of His kindness, intentionality, courage, and love.

The Gospels are filled with examples of Jesus treating outcasts with love and dignity:

- When no one else would come within ten cubits of him, Jesus touched a man with leprosy and instantly cleansed him of the disease. The man could then show himself to the priests and be welcomed back into society (Matthew 8:1–3; Luke 5:12–16).
- Jesus stopped in the middle of a large crowd to recognize the faith of a woman with a bleeding disease. In front of everyone, He applauded her belief that healed her of the disorder that had left her penniless and in pain for twelve years (Matthew 9:20–22; Mark 5:25–34; Luke 8:43–48).
- After listening patiently to the persistent pleas of a Canaanite mother, Jesus granted her request and expelled the demons from her daughter (Matthew 15:21–28; Mark 7:24–30).
- Jesus invited Mary Magdalene, a woman once possessed by seven demons, to follow Him. She not only became one of His ministry partners, but she was the first person Jesus revealed Himself to after rising from the grave (Matthew 27:56, 61, 28:1; Mark 15:47, 16:1, 9; Luke 8:2, 24:10; John 19:25, 20:1, 16–18).
- At a dinner party hosted by Simon the Pharisee, Jesus honored the gift of an immoral woman as she washed his feet and anointed Him with perfume. This was her most prized possession and a true sacrifice—yet she gave it freely and lovingly to Jesus. Jesus shocks everyone

in the room when He offers her a gift in return—forgiveness for her sins. Jesus is showing them that no one is too dirty to be made clean again, and no one is beyond the reach of His love (Luke 7:36–50).

The Woman at the Well

One of my favorite interactions in Scripture is between Jesus and the woman at the well, as recorded in John 4:1–42. This story shows us that Jesus doesn't shy away from people living in messy circumstances. He doesn't keep things "PC" and tidy. He rocks the boat. He does the unexpected. He goes out of His way to be sure we have a personal encounter with Him, even when we feel like an outcast . . . especially when we feel like an outcast.

This story highlights two valuable lessons about Jesus and His ministry:

- Jesus breaks down cultural, racial, and religious walls.
- Jesus uses the broken to bring healing and wholeness to the world.

On his way back to Galilee from Judea, Jesus routes His followers on a path that would take them through a town any other group of Jews would have avoided at all costs—Samaria. The Jews and Samaritans hated each other. But Jesus was about to shake up the ground on this longstanding rivalry. It was just about lunchtime, so Jesus sent the disciples to town to get food. He headed to Jacob's well to rest from the midday sun. It is no coincidence that a Samaritan woman came to that very spot at that very time to get water for the day.

With sweat dripping from her brow and shame stirring in her heart, Jesus asks her for a drink. Wait, what?

He knew this went against all cultural norms. Jews didn't associate with Samaritans, much less unclean Samaritan women. But Jesus knew her story. He knew she had been shunned by society because of her life choices. He knew all the other women from the village came together in the cool of the morning while this woman walked alone in the hottest part of the day to avoid their inevitable scorn and ridicule. He also knew

He had something to offer her that would change her life and the lives of many others if she chose to accept it.

She doesn't hold back her disapproval and shock at Jesus's request. But when Jesus tells her that He has living water that will quench her thirst forever, she begs Him for a drink. Hope bubbles up in her heart as she imagines never having to climb that blasted hill again. But before she can taste it, Jesus asks her to go and get her husband. Aaaaand, bubble popped.

Jesus knew she wasn't married. And when He starts spouting off all the things she'd ever done, He wasn't trying to shame her. He was trying to show her who He was. He was the Messiah. And the moment she realized He really was the Christ, everything changed. She didn't even remember to grab her water bucket before running back to her village to tell everyone about Jesus.

And here's the part that has me flat on the floor. When she runs back into town to tell everyone about this man who told her everything she had ever done, they drop what they're doing, follow her up that hill, and then beg Him to stay in their village. The very people who had shunned her were the same people who followed her to Jesus. The one who had been unwelcome at the well was the one who led her whole town to the living well of life.

I just can't get over this!

Time and again in Scripture, Jesus breaks down cultural, racial, and religious walls and uses broken people with messy pasts to bring healing and wholeness to the people around them. Keep this in mind the next time you read the command in Scripture to "fear not!" Remember, it's not there to shame you. It's there to remind you that Jesus, the Messiah, has come to set you free. He will pursue you no matter how messy your life looks or how hardened your heart may be to the goodness of God.

Hope for the Weary

My struggles with mental health have left me feeling like an outcast more times than I can count. Even within the church, people with good intentions have left me feeling unseen, unheard, unloved, and unwelcome. Bad theology tempted me to believe that faith in Jesus cures everything, science is bad, and mental illness is only something the desperately deranged deal with. But the story of the woman at the well, and the countless other times Jesus gives value to those who were told they were worthless, reminds me that Jesus can use anyone and anything to bring hope and healing into this world.

For me, He used a boy I had a crush on in the eighth grade to lead me to His well of never-ending love. The woman at the well climbed the hill full of shame, regret, and exhaustion, but after she met Jesus, she sprinted down full of hope, love, and exhilaration. I walked into a youth group looking for the admiration of a boy, but I walked out holding the lasting love of the Savior of the world.

Knowing Jesus does not mean our lives will be pain free. Jesus prepares us for the fact that difficulties are inevitable (John 16:33). The difference is that by knowing Him and trusting Him as our Savior, we are given the help of the Holy Spirit as we face the trials of this world (John 14:17, 26). Christ offers us hope during our deepest sorrows and through our greatest challenges.

(RE)FRAME IT

Let's take a moment to identify how our beliefs affect our behavior, which lies need to be replaced with truth, and what steps we can take to move toward whole health.

WORLDVIEW: How has my upbringing affected my mindset?
Did your family practice faith or attend a church when you were a child? When did you first hear about God, Jesus, the Holy Spirit, and the Bible?

BELIEFS: How has my worldview filtered what I believe to be true?
How did your family's faith or lack of faith impact you? What did you believe to be true about the God of the Bible as a child? What words would you use to describe your understanding of Christianity as a child?

VALUES: How have my beliefs framed what I value?

How have your beliefs about God impacted your view of yourself and others? What external expectations were placed on you? What internal battles do you face?

 CHOICES: How have my values influenced my choices?

How have your choices been impacted by your faith or lack of faith? Your family's faith or lack of faith? Have you been led by love or shame? Grace or intolerance? Reverence or wrath? Do you have a safe space to work through your questions, doubts, and fears?

 RESULT: How have my choices helped or hurt me and those around me?

How has anxiety, depression, or chronic illness impacted your faith? What steps can you take today to clean the lens of your faith so you can see Jesus more clearly? Who can you reach out to for help?

If you've never put your faith in Jesus, what better time to do that than right now? No matter where you've been, Jesus is ready to walk with you today. Like the woman at the well, He loves you just as you are. He's available to you and cheering for you. All He asks from us is to recognize that we are sinners in need of a Savior and that He is the one who came to set us free. Jesus gave His life for ours, not just so we wouldn't die apart from Him but so that we could live in freedom with Him. If you believe that, tell Him that you accept His sacrifice for the atonement of your sins and trust Him as your Savior. And then allow the Holy Spirit to fill you with all you need to follow Him and learn to walk with Him through this marvelously messy life and all of eternity.

PRAY ABOUT IT

Jehovah M'Kaddesh, you are the God who sanctifies. Thank you for loving me so much that you offered your own son as a sacrifice so that my relationship with you could be restored. May I never forget how truly amazing this is.

Jesus, you are the Messiah—the one the world waited for and the one I want to follow.

Thank you for coming as a humble baby to bring hope and healing to all of humanity. Thank you for assuming responsibility for my failures and debt. I am free because of you. Thank you for lifting my head from shame. Thank you for welcoming the outcasts and giving dignity to sinners like me. Thank you for showing me example after example in your Word that there is no one too far gone to receive your love and offer of forgiveness.

Thank you for promising to be with me through every circumstance of this life. Every joy. Every pain. And every other messy, marvelous thing in between. Give me faith to trust your process. Like the woman at the well, use me to lead others to your well of living water.

In the name of the Father, the Son, and the Holy Spirit, amen.

MESSterpiece REMINDER:
I may be a mess, but Jesus can use anyone and anything to bring hope and healing into this world.

Chapter 2

MELTDOWNS, PANIC ATTACKS, AND THE PERPLEXING PROVISION OF GOD

The Spirit of the Sovereign Lord is on me, because the Lord has anointed me to proclaim good news to the poor.

Isaiah 61:1

Trigger warning: This chapter delves into the intrusive thoughts of anxiety, depression, panic disorder, and suicidal thoughts. This may stir up bad memories or hard realities for you. If you are struggling, remember you are not alone, and there is no shame in reaching out for help. You matter, and you are fully loved by God in the middle of this mess.

I'D ALREADY MICROWAVED MY COFFEE three times that morning. Yet there it sat on the counter—cold again. And I needed that coffee. I couldn't remember the last time I'd had a good night's sleep—much less brushed my teeth, washed my hair, or shaved my legs. Tired didn't even begin to describe how I felt.

My one-year-old ginger boy was teething and fussy. As I tried to soothe him with the famous bounce and sway, my daughter entered the room with a hair-raising shrill that set my nerves on fire. She was three, and she was mad. About what exactly, I can't recall. What I do remember is feeling trapped. Feeling helpless. Feeling so overwhelmed and exhausted that I didn't know if we'd all make it through the day intact.

35

The tension in my body boiled hot as my baby fussed and my toddler shrilled. And then it happened. With the force of a ninja warrior, I watched the last ounce of my sanity leave my body, and I screamed at the top of my lungs, "Just stop! I can't take this anymore!" I felt the baby jolt in my arms, and the shock on my daughter's face brought me to my knees.

All three of us were now a puddle of tears on the floor. As I wept, I waged war on myself: "Andrea, what is wrong with you? How could you explode on your kids like that? God has entrusted you to take care of them, and you are failing. You're such a terrible mom!"

I felt like a child stuck in an adult's body. I needed a parent, but now I was the parent. I needed to be nurtured, but now I was the one everyone depended on to nurture them. I couldn't get my act together no matter how hard I tried, and they deserved so much more than this.

Whispers from darkness lured me into believing my family would be better off without me. Suddenly I was sure my husband would be happier with a different wife, and my kids would be healthier with a different mom. Desperately confused, I cried out to God from the depth of my soul: *How can I know the hope of Christ but feel so hopeless? How can I be holding everything I ever wanted and feel this way? What gives, God?*

I see now that even our blessings can feel burdensome when things are off balance. And things had been off for a while.

The Panic Attack

Motherhood can certainly intensify your senses and push you to the edge of your sanity. I've always been a highly sensitive and emotionally driven person, but this was different. Something was not right. Fear began to debilitate me. Calamity was around every corner. I could hardly go anywhere or do anything without intrusive thoughts sabotaging my mind. In the car, I'd have scenes flash in my mind of us all being killed in an accident. When my husband prepared dinner using raw chicken, I was convinced we'd all end up with salmonella poisoning and die. Any random sound in the house was someone trying to break in and hurt us.

I was constantly on edge.

The only thing that helped to drown out the doom and despair—if only for a moment—was food. So I took up emotional binge eating. For weeks, the hazy fog of my existence was kept afloat with a steady flow of oversized chai lattes and daily trips to Krispy Kreme. I paid in cash so there was no evidence of our secret rendezvous. I was like a prisoner in my own body, a marionette being controlled by an invisible puppeteer.

One stormy Friday morning in mid-February, I felt more off than usual. After tucking my kids in for their afternoon nap, I sat on the couch, threw a blanket over my legs, pulled out my phone, and typed my symptoms into the search bar of WebMD. Excellent plan, I know.

As my fingers swiped the screen, a strange numbness suddenly shot up my arms. Blood rushed from my head, making my living room feel like a funhouse mirror—distorted, off-balance, and sideways. My lungs gasped for air, but I couldn't seem to get enough. The pounding of my heart seemed in sync with the countdown of a detonated bomb eager to explode. Hands shaking and voice trembling, I called my neighbor to see if she was home. Poor thing was in the car when she answered.

"I think I'm having a heart attack!"

"Oh my God! I'll call 911 and tell Jacob to come over when he gets home in a minute!"

Just then the dog started barking. With a glance at the time, I realized the mail person was close by. With wobbly legs and blurry eyes, the ten feet from my living room to my front door seemed like ten miles. I turned the deadbolt, opened the door, and screamed for help. Collapsed in the doorway, I called my husband in a panic, terrified the kids would wake up to find me lifeless on the floor. "I don't know what's wrong. I'm so scared. I love you so much."

To my relief, the firefighters arrived quickly, and I handed one of them my phone to speak to my husband. After giving me a once over, I heard something along the lines of: "Sir, I don't think your wife is in a life-threatening situation, but I do want to get her to the hospital ASAP for an evaluation. How soon can you be home?" Since it would take him twenty minutes, the EMT told him they would take me by ambulance and to meet us at the hospital.

Before I could blink, I sat on a stretcher headed to the ER. I caught a glimpse of my neighbor's husband in the doorway as they wheeled me out. I silently prayed, *God, please let me walk back through these doors. Let me live to see my babies again.*

My husband, Eric, was soon by my side, and hours of tests and tears lay before us at the hospital. But the pokes and prods yielded no results. Everything was "normal." I was "fine." They discharged me from the ER with the conclusion that I must have just been stressed. What in the world?

I crawled into bed that night confused, embarrassed, and angry. But when I woke up the next morning, God brought a recent conversation with a friend to mind. We had been chatting on Facebook Messenger, so I sat down at my computer to re-read the message. Little did I know, God had been preparing the way to help me navigate something that hadn't happened yet.

A few weeks before my ER fiasco, I felt God asking me to reach out to the women in my MOPS group at church for support. We had a private Facebook group, so I shared my struggles there:

Andrea Coletta Nyberg
January 29, 2015

Hey mamas, I need to be brave and get personal for a moment: I'm struggling with severe anxiety right now (including extreme sensitivity to sound, lack of energy and fear). I originally mistook my symptoms for depression but after lots of research understand it's definitely anxiety. I'm curious if anyone else is dealing with/has dealt with this and how you found relief and/or ways to cope. I'm beginning to clearly see this affecting my kids and I'm heartbroken. Thanks for your listening ears and support!

28 Comments

👍 Like   💬 Comment

Twenty-eight women replied within the thread with stories of a similar struggle. Many others reached out privately to share resources that had helped them navigate difficult seasons. Rebekah's message—the one

God brought to mind that morning—would literally change the trajectory of my life.

Rebekah had just begun an internship at a local Christian Counseling Center here in San Jose. She assured me I was not alone in my struggles and that reaching out to talk to someone may prove helpful. Included in her note were the names of three therapists she had come to know and trust. Should I ever feel inclined to reach out, I had somewhere to start.

After enduring a fruitless night at the ER, I decided to give Rebekah's recommendation a try. I called the first name on the list, and a woman named Janie answered. After explaining what I'd just gone through, we made an appointment to see each other Monday afternoon.

On the day of my first therapy session, a tall, thin woman with short brown hair and a friendly smile greeted me at the door. We shook hands, and she invited me to have a seat on her gray couch with oversized throw pillows. A box of tissues sat ready on the table, and the leaves of a birch tree danced in the breeze just outside the window. She handed me a printout and asked me to put a checkmark next to the items that resonated with how I felt. Check, check, check. Every single item on the page resounded, "Yes! This is me!"

The information I found in my furious internet searches a few weeks earlier had only scratched the surface of understanding what was happening in my body. The ER staff focused solely on my physical health, but Janie was able to zone in on my mental health and the visceral effects it was creating. Within the first fifteen minutes of sitting with her, versus the hours spent at the hospital two nights before, we discovered I was battling generalized anxiety disorder and clinical depression. And the thing that felt like a heart attack was actually a panic attack.

The weight that lifted from my body at that moment was tangible. The chaos had a name. And Janie had the tools to diagnose and treat it.

If you're not familiar with the disorders of anxiety and depression, allow me a moment to get textbook savvy with you on these illnesses. Whether to better understand your own symptoms or the struggles of someone you love, having a common language is invaluable when discussing these disorders.

What Are Anxiety and Depression?

All of our emotions are good, God-given tools to help us navigate the variety of experiences we will encounter throughout our lives. Things happen both within our control and outside of our control that throw off the delicate chemical makeup of our bodies. This can result in healthy emotions—like fear, sadness, and anger—morphing into unhealthy conditions—like anxiety, depression, and panic attacks. Scientific explanations for anxiety and depression range from genetics (DNA), gender, personality type, unhealthy expectations, constant stress and pressure to perform, substance abuse, trauma, neglect, hormone imbalances, physical illness, misfiring of chemicals in the brain, or a combination of these or other factors.[4]

Fear or Anxiety?

Fear is our body's natural protection mechanism with a unique fight-or-flight mode that gives us a rush of adrenaline to either fight the danger in front of us or get the heck away from it. Fear is a healthy and appropriate response to danger, both real and perceived. It is also an inherent response to issues and events that don't promise the outcome we desire.

It's perfectly natural to be nervous about an important project at work, a new baby, the responsibilities that come with raising a child, the inability to have the baby your heart desires, a pending biopsy, going after a new dream, or letting go of something familiar. Each of these scenarios can invoke an innate sense of fear. Even good things can be scary, and life is full of curveballs that catch us off guard.

We encounter problems within our fight-or-flight framework when our bodies don't recognize the difference between a real threat and a perceived danger.[5] Fear can morph into an anxiety disorder when our body's natural fight-or-flight mechanism fails to disengage. If you find yourself in a constant state of worry affecting your day-to-day life, you may be experiencing *anxiety disorder.*[6]

Symptoms of Anxiety Disorder

- irritability

- racing thoughts
- being easily startled
- fear of making the wrong decision
- feelings of impending doom
- restlessness
- difficulty concentrating or zoning out
- heart palpitations
- nausea
- insomnia

Panic Attacks

Panic attacks are sudden eruptions of intense fear—whether or not you're in real danger—that produce extreme and frightening physical reactions. You may feel like you're having a heart attack, a stroke, or even dying. Dealing with these symptoms can turn your world upside down. But take heart—panic attacks are not life threatening. If you've had one, there's a chance you live in fear of having another one. You may knowingly or unknowingly begin to avoid places, belongings, or even people that stir up memories of your first attack. Unfortunately, this can lead to phobias and other disorders. Frustrating, I know. If you're having frequent attacks, or living in constant fear of having another one, you may be dealing with *panic disorder.*[7]

Symptoms of a Panic Attack

- sense of imminent danger or catastrophe
- fear of losing control
- fear of death for you or a loved one
- fast, pounding heart rate
- sweating
- trembling or shaking
- shortness of breath or tightness in your throat
- chills
- hot flashes

- nausea
- abdominal cramping
- chest pain
- headache
- dizziness, lightheadedness, or faintness
- numbness or tingling sensation
- feeling detached from reality

Many report their symptoms starting in their late teens and early twenties. You may be at higher risk if you smoke; drink excessive amounts of caffeine; have a family history of panic attacks or panic disorder; have endured a traumatic event, such as a sexual assault or a serious accident; or recently experienced a major life event, like divorce, a death in the family, a serious diagnosis, or a new baby. If you think you may be dealing with panic disorder, talk to your doctor about what resources are available to you. In addition to therapy and medication, many hospitals and community centers offer classes that discuss coping techniques.

Sadness or Depression?

Sadness is your body's natural response to loss, change, or something not turning out how you hoped it would. It's healthy and appropriate to feel sad when you're struggling: not receiving the promotion you worked so hard for, having a fallout with a friend or family member, finalizing a divorce, enduring another false pregnancy test, receiving the diagnosis you were dreading, or saying goodbye to someone you love far too soon.

Sadness deserves a seat of honor at the table of our lives. She should not be reprimanded to move on, get over it, or buck up. She should not be hidden under a blanket of shallow comfort, unable to offer the true gift she was designed to give us. Grief must be felt and lived and allowed breathing room. And it's important to be in tune with your body.

If it's been a couple of weeks and you're still so sad that you can't enjoy the activities, people, or places you usually would, your sadness may be morphing into *clinical depression*.[8] It may be time to seek help.

Symptoms of Depression:

- fatigue
- loss of interest
- change in sleeping and eating habits
- difficulty concentrating
- apathy in making decisions
- low self-esteem
- feelings of hopelessness
- thoughts of suicide

New moms may experience a period of "baby blues" during the first two weeks after bringing their baby home from the hospital. But if it's been more than a couple of weeks and you are still having unexplained crying spells, questioning whether you have what it takes to care for your baby, not interested in things you usually enjoy, struggling to make decisions, unable to rest when your baby is napping, or having thoughts of harming yourself or your baby, you may be dealing with *postpartum depression.*[9]

Please know you're not alone. Talk to someone about how you're feeling, and don't be ashamed to get medical and professional help to assist you in finding your new normal.

Unhealthy Ways We Cope with Anxiety and Depression

Many of us turn to food, sleep, sex, alcohol, excessive spending, or TV for quick comfort, satisfaction, or sense of control when we're hurting. These questions will help you take an inventory of the state of your mental and emotional health:

- Do I enjoy the people, places, and activities that usually bring me joy?
- Am I abusing food, exercise, sex/pornography, alcohol, or drugs?
- Am I staying late at work to avoid my family?
- Is my fear of failure keeping me from completing tasks and interacting with the people I care about?
- Have I become complacent in my daily tasks?
- Am I self-harming? Cutting? Not eating? Overeating?
- Do I fantasize about falling sleeping and never waking up?

- Do I question if I'm too much of a burden to my family and think they'd be better off without me?
- Am I getting my personal affairs in order with plans to end my life?

If you think you may be experiencing depression or suicidal thoughts, please call your doctor or the National Suicide Prevention Lifeline at 988. You are not alone, and there is no shame in reaching out for help to overcome these diseases of the mind.

One of the hardest parts of living with anxiety and depression is its unpredictable nature. The inability to predict when and where another panic attack will hit. The sinking feeling of waking up to that knot in the pit of your stomach, unsure of what triggered the depression this time. The uncertainty of how long you'll be down and out.

This is hard. And it's okay to feel all the feelings . . . the disappointment, sadness, and anger. The hope of Jesus meets us in our hopelessness—even when we can't quite grasp it. One day we will experience a reality void of sadness, grief, and agony. First Peter 5:10 (TLB) assures us, "After you have suffered a little while, our God, who is full of kindness through Christ, will give you his eternal glory. He personally will come and pick you up, and set you firmly in place, and make you stronger than ever." Until that day, we live by faith in Christ, who is with us in the pain and through the storms.

(RE)FRAME IT

Let's take a moment to identify how our beliefs affect our behavior, which lies need to be replaced with truth, and what steps we can take to move toward whole health.

WORLDVIEW: How has my upbringing affected my mindset?
Was mental health talked about in your home as a child? In your place of worship? If so, what was the general vibe and tone in discussions about anxiety, depression, bipolar disorder, and other matters of the mind?

BELIEFS: How has my worldview filtered what I believe to be true?
What did you believe to be true about people diagnosed with mental illness? Was it suggested that people with mental illness were "crazy" and should be institutionalized? Or were these disorders discussed with dignity and understanding? If you struggle or know someone who struggles with a mental illness, how have these initial beliefs impacted your identity and empathy toward others?

VALUES: How have my beliefs framed what I value?
Were you taught to value good health as a child? Was being healthy, safe, and happy seen as the blessings of God in your home growing up? Did you associate or observe from your caregivers that poor health, danger, and being unhappy were directly correlated to your faith and favor with God? How have these values impacted you?

CHOICES: How have my values influenced my choices?
How has your understanding or misunderstanding of mental illness impacted your choices and conversations around the topic? Are you judgmental, afraid, ashamed, intrigued?

RESULT: How have my choices helped or hurt me and those around me?
What would you go back and say or do differently knowing what you know now? What do you want others to know and understand about mental health and what it looks like to struggle with a disorder of the mind? Who can you share your story with today?

PRAY ABOUT IT

Jehovah-Jireh, you are the God who provides. Thank you for countless ways you are pursuing me, loving me, and offering me help for the many hurts I carry—even the ones I've caused. Please reveal any unhealthy mindsets or beliefs keeping me from experiencing your love, care, and direction. Help me not be afraid or ashamed to pursue professional help.

Give me eyes to see you. When anxiety fills my mind and hijacks my body, give me ears to hear your words of peace being spoken over me. When depression lures me toward the darkness and I can't see the light at the end of the tunnel, give me faith to trust you. When I'm weary, confused, feeling hopeless, and ashamed, give me faith to follow you. Give me the courage to connect in community, share my story, and accept the gift of friendship—even though I'm afraid to come as I am.

Help me believe in what I can't yet see. Help me stay faithful even when you don't offer the healing I desire in the way I desire it. Help me not to miss the many ways you are speaking to me. Give me eyes to see you, ears to hear you, and a heart to know you.

In the name of the Father, the Son, and the Holy Spirit, amen.

MESSterpiece REMINDER:
I can trust God, my Provider, past the limits of my understanding.

Chapter 3

IT'S NOT FAIR!

He has sent me to bind up the brokenhearted...
Isaiah 61:1

BEING THE HIGHLY SENSITIVE, DEEPLY intuitive, grace-driven woman I am, I naturally married a highly logical, deeply rational, truth-driven man. Help! Ideally, we'd be the yin to each other's yang. But the reality is, it's a hard-swinging pendulum of head versus heart every day over here. God really does have a sense of humor when it comes to matchmaking.

Eric and I met in 2005 when I made a cross-country move from my hometown of Memphis, Tennessee, to the hills of Mill Valley, California, to attend Golden Gate Seminary. Two summers before, I spent the summer in Santa Cruz on a project with Cru—the college ministry formerly known as Campus Crusade for Christ—and fell madly in love with the West Coast. When God made it clear that he wanted me to attend seminary after college, I was beside myself to find there was a Baptist seminary in Northern California, just ninety minutes from my beloved banana slug beach town!

Eric had already been a student at the seminary for over a year when I arrived, so he was familiar with the area. I wanted to put together a collection of photos to show my family back home, and Eric knew a place where we'd get views of the bay area spanning from San Francisco to Oakland. Amazing! There was just one teensy weensy problem—this would involve hiking a literal mountain. And I'm not what one would describe as outdoorsy.

Now don't get me wrong—I love nature. I just don't want it to crawl on me, buzz near me, or slither by me. At the time, I had been on only one other hike that I could recall, and that adventure left me with a bruised tailbone and a deeper seeded phobia of bees. So I had been less than eager to willingly insert myself into a situation like that again. The problem was, I liked Eric. A lot. So I mustered up my *fake it till you make it* moxie and gratefully accepted his invitation to spend the day with him—climbing a mountain.

I changed my clothes three times the day of our hike. I couldn't decide: jeans or yoga pants? Boots or tennis shoes? Long sleeves or short? This was not a date, by the way. Just an outing of two new friends on a mission to get some amazing photos of Marin County to show my family back in Memphis. I went with yoga pants, tennis shoes, and short sleeves, in case you're like me and need closure!

The beginning of the hike was easy as we tread over dusty gravel on level ground. But the grade quickly got steeper, requiring more thought and energy. Mt. Tamalpais is 2,572 feet in elevation, and our goal was to make it to the old lookout and touch the door. (This had become a popular tradition among visitors, so it would have been a shame not to join in.) The climb had my muscles straining to push through and my mind a bit unsteady on the unknown terrain. But together, we made it to the top, scaled those final steps to touch the door of the lookout point, documented our achievement with a photo, then found a spot to sit and enjoy the fruit of our labor—a 360-degree view of the beautiful bay.

We spent the next hour or so eating, talking, and taking those photos we had journeyed to capture. I posed with the wind in my hair as Eric played photographer. He was easy to talk to, and we quickly discovered how much we had in common. He accompanied his grandmother to the symphony growing up. So had I. I served as a youth leader at my church during college. He had too. He traveled to Romania the summer before on a mission trip. I had been to Romania twice in 2001. Our shared love of music, art, and culture made for meaningful conversation, and I didn't want our mountaintop experience to end. But alas, we needed to allow ourselves plenty of time to get back down before sunset.

Let me just say that for me, going up is much easier than coming down. The rush of adrenaline at the challenge of arriving at my desired destination keeps me moving on the incline. But coming down? It just makes me weak in the knees. And not in the way Eric had begun to make me feel.

Eric went ahead of me and extended his hand for support on the steep steps down. I'm certain this was much slower than his natural pace, but for my sake, he was a generous guide. I felt safe following his lead. Where he stepped, I stepped. We made it to the bottom in one piece, with no sprained ankles or bee stings, just as the sun was slipping beneath the horizon. As vibrant strokes of orange, purple, and blue burst across the sky, a sense of serenity filled my soul. And I had a sneaky suspicion that this would not be my last adventure with Eric.

His Beloved

Eric and I had been spending more time together, so I didn't think much of it when he came to visit me in the girls' dorm that chilly Wednesday morning in mid-December. We walked to the lobby to talk, but to my surprise, he sat down at the piano and set a crinkled sheet of paper against the music stand. My heart started beating hard in my chest. Why was he sitting at the piano?

He explained that he hadn't been able to get our conversation from the day before out of his mind. I had vulnerably shared my ongoing struggle of feeling like too much and yet not enough. He woke up in the middle of the night with the lyrics of a song ringing in his mind and was not able to get back to sleep until he located the sheet music so he could share the song . . . with me. Cue the tears.

Eric's fingers drifted across those black and white ivories, and he began to sing. His voice resonated to the depths of my soul, reawakening me to the truth of who I am and whose I am. "Your Beloved" by Vineyard Music speaks to the fact that I'm God's beloved. The one who put the stars in the heavens and told the ocean waves where to stop calls me His own. He takes pride in me and loves me as I am, without shame or reservation. Wow. You can view the beautiful lyrics at:

https://genius.com/Vineyard-worship-your-beloved-lyrics

Eric had not only taken my words to heart but held my pain with me. He not only felt God's nudge to share words of truth with me but woke up in the middle of the night to find the sheet music to a song from the nineties so he could sing it to me. Y'all!

We started dating in January and were engaged that September. On June 2, 2007, the lyrics of "Your Beloved" filled the room as I walked down the aisle to become Mrs. Eric Nyberg. It was a nearly perfect day filled with worship, laughter, dancing, family, and friends.

At first, the road was easy. Our newfound love had us swooning and smitten. We went out of our way to impress each other and show our affection and admiration. But as we made the climb into married life, things got harder, and the sweat from the journey had us a little less infatuated and a little more annoyed with each other. What once came easy now took intention. More and more often, instead of leaning in toward each other for support and strength, we turned against each other. Especially after the accident.

We had only been married for three months, and I was on my way to work. The light had just turned green, and I hadn't even taken my foot off the brake when I felt the crash. The car behind me, which was coming over a hill, hit me at about 35 mph. Because of the angle of the collision, the front end of her car picked up the back end of mine and slammed me down again. Oddly enough, neither car looked damaged, but I quickly realized my body had absorbed the brunt of the impact.

We exchanged information and went our separate ways. At first, I just felt pain in my neck, but I was otherwise okay. But as the morning went on, the pain grew stronger, and my ability to move around became more impaired. I left work early and went to see a local chiropractor. Some imaging showed a whiplash injury, which they assured me could be effectively treated with their services. But the imaging was unable to detect the many complications this injury would create.

To make matters worse, the woman who hit me gave me an old business card to a company she hadn't worked at for more than seven years. Since I failed to get her license plate number (big mistake!) and she had given faulty information, which made her untraceable, I had to file a claim against my own insurance. Even though I was not at fault, the insurance company, which I worked for at the time, made me jump through numerous hoops to prove my injury. It was a nightmare. She got off scot-free while our world got turned upside down.

The first week after the accident, I couldn't bend forward without excruciating pain. Eric had to get in the shower with me to help me bathe. While this may sound like the stuff of newlyweds, let me assure you, it was anything but pleasurable. The migraines hit next. Any amount of light or sound pierced my eyes and head, so Eric covered the windows and tiptoed around our four-hundred-square-foot apartment while I lay on the couch, begging God to ease the pain.

I tried medication after medication, but they brought more side effects than relief. Some sent shock waves through my body, while others caused tightness in my neck and throat, making me feel like I was being strangled. So that was a no-go. I went into the chiropractic office two to three days a week for several months—even adding in massage therapy with hopes it would help—but the pain persisted. I was losing hope but managed to gain fifty pounds that year. It was a rough start to our "happily ever after."

Not Fair

The tension took a toll on our relationship. Marriage was supposed to be a partnership, but my injury drastically tipped the scale on a fair division of labor. Just leaning forward to wash my hands hurt my neck, so forget washing the dishes or doing the laundry. And when the migraines hit, I'd be out for days at a time. Nearly all the household chores and daily duties fell solely on Eric's shoulders, and what was meant to be a joint venture was now a one-man show.

We felt ill-equipped to handle how my injury had rerouted our lives. Days turned into weeks, and weeks turned into months. And even though he loves me fiercely, Eric's brain is hard-wired with a sense of right and wrong, black and white, just and unjust. Our current predicament was not fair, but there was nothing either of us could do about it. When we vowed to love each other "in sickness and in health," we had no idea how quickly our commitment would get put to the test.

Sometimes Eric would remind me that he wasn't mad at me, he was mad at the circumstances. But his anger sure was flying my direction. And my reactions to him grew more intense and defensive. Not only that, but I became wildly jealous of his interactions with other women. In my eyes, any woman who appeared capable was now competition. Compared to a broken mess like me, they seemed to have everything I didn't. And I was certain he was going to wake up one day, realize he'd had enough, and leave.

I was broken, and now I was afraid my marriage was going to break. I felt unlovable, and he felt unappreciated. Instead of proactively facing the problem side by side, we played the blame game and allowed bitterness to turn us against each other. Bitterness is like a disease that spreads quickly unless it's nipped in the bud. Unfortunately for us, we let it fester, and fifteen years into our marriage, we are still digging up the diseased roots from our first years as husband and wife.

Thief

As the years passed, more health problems emerged. Before the accident, I already had hypothyroidism, digestive disorders, and endometriosis. Now I had migraines and fibromyalgia. And if that wasn't enough, anxiety and depression would join the party a few years later. Seriously, what gives?

Chronic illness is such a thief, isn't it? It breaks into our bodies and steals such valuable assets. One minute, everything is fine. The next minute, everything we hoped for seems to be slipping through our fingers. The joy and adventure we long for are trapped under despair and fatigue. Tension rises with our loved ones because it's hard to understand invisible pain. Just like my car when I got rear-ended, things may look fine on the outside to those around us, but under the surface, pain is crushing us. The impact of invisible illness rarely bears physical battle scars, so it's hard for others to understand how debilitating it can be.

Sometimes we don't feel like anyone takes our pain seriously.

We have to become our own advocates by learning all we can about our symptoms so we face a fighting chance of getting relief or, at minimum, a treatment plan. It's exhausting, lonely, and discouraging. So we pop some pain meds, hunker down under the heating pad, and find a rom-com—or three—to watch. We have a pity party for ourselves as we ponder all the things we missed out on because we're sick . . . again. This is not what our lives were supposed to look like. Nor is it what our loved ones signed up for. Our marriages, motherhood, and ministries are all impacted by our health, and we often have to dig deep to find the joy, joy, joy we know is down in our hearts.

If you know what I'm talking about, you're in good company.

And again, it's okay to feel all the feelings. The disappointment, sadness, and anger. This is hard. And—the love of our Father meets us right in the middle of this mess.

Unfailing Love

I deeply resonate with the psalms of the Bible. Cries for mercy. Pleas for forgiveness. Struggles with lust, anger, pain, and fear. God was so good to include these in His Word. Not only do the psalms prove that we can bring anything to the Father in prayer, but they also showcase that God uses broken people to accomplish His plans.

While most psalms were written by David, Psalm 73 is one of twelve composed by the choir director, Asaph. It speaks to the despair that bitterness and envy create but also to the unfailing love of a God who holds onto us, even when we don't deserve it. And it's one of my favorites.

> Truly God is good to Israel, to those whose hearts are pure. But as for me, I almost lost my footing. My feet were slipping, and I was almost gone. For I envied the proud when I saw them prosper despite their wickedness. They seem to live such painless lives; their bodies are so healthy and strong. They don't have troubles like other people; they're not plagued with problems like everyone else. . . . Did I keep my heart pure for nothing? Did I keep myself innocent for no reason? I get nothing but

trouble all day long; every morning brings me pain. . . . Then I realized that my heart was bitter, and I was all torn up inside. I was so foolish and ignorant—I must have seemed like a sense-less animal to you. Yet I still belong to you; you hold my right hand. You guide me with your counsel, leading me to a glorious destiny. Whom have I in heaven but you? I desire you more than anything on earth. My health may fail, and my spirit may grow weak, but God remains the strength of my heart; he is mine forever. (Psalm 73:1–5, 13–14, 21–26 NLT)

Can you relate to Asaph's bitterness and envy? I sure can. It's easy for me to harden my heart toward people who don't know the burden of chronic illness personally—even people I love. Thankfully, my strug-gle with bitterness and envy does not keep God from loving me. It does, however, serve as the gauge of how healthy my mind and heart are. Like the check engine light on my car, bitterness and envy are warning lights that my faith needs a tune-up.

As I think about this, I'm brought back to the lobby of the girls' dorm on that chilly Wednesday morning when Eric sat down at the piano to sing truth over my soul. Even when I feel like too much and not enough, I am beloved by the God of the universe. Even when I feel broken and unlovable, I am the divinely crafted, chosen daughter of the King.

The same is true for you, friend.

Even when our feet are slipping and all seems lost, we are God's beloved. Even when bitterness and envy poison our disposition, we are God's beloved. Even when we doubt His goodness, we are God's beloved. Even when our health fails and our spirits are weak, we are forever His beloved.

May you find strength and comfort in His love today.

(RE)FRAME IT

Let's take a moment to identify how our beliefs affect our behavior, which lies need to be replaced with truth, and what steps we can take to move toward whole health.

📷 **WORLDVIEW: How has my upbringing affected my mindset?**
How was conflict handled in your home? By yelling? Shutting down? Running away? Talking it out?

◎ **BELIEFS: How has my worldview filtered what I believe to be true?**
Think of an instance in your life when something completely unexpected turned everything upside down. How did those involved (including yourself, if applicable) respond? Did people start pointing fingers and blaming each other? Or were things worked out calmly with a sense that everyone was on the same team? How does this impact your understanding of how relationships work?

◎ **VALUES: How have my beliefs framed what I value?**
How have your early interactions with conflict management, or lack thereof, impacted your relationships? As a child? Teen? Adult? Do you fight to win every argument? Do you acquiesce to avoid conflict?

✴ **CHOICES: How have my values influenced my choices?**
Has something that seems completely unfair produced feelings of bitterness, envy, jealousy, or anger within you? How are these feelings impacting your most important relationships?

🖼 **RESULT: How have my choices helped or hurt me and those around me?**
How does Psalm 73 land for you? What is something you can take away from knowing that no matter what, you belong to God, and He will strengthen and guide you? What do you sense God is asking you to bring to Him today that is causing turmoil in your soul?

PRAY ABOUT IT

Yahweh-Shammah, you are the Lord who is present. You are the God who came near and the one who will never leave me or forsake me. Thank you for your faithfulness to me no matter how faithful I remain to you.

Thank you for calling me your beloved, even when my faith falters and my heart is hardened. Thank you for loving me even when I'm defensive and bitter. Thank you for the people in my life who also love me when I'm at my worst.

This is hard. I feel robbed of so much because of pain and illness. This all just seems so unfair.

Yet I know you're with me. I know you're working things out in ways I can't see on the surface yet. As I bring my burdens to your feet, tune my heart to sing your praise, even in the middle of this trial.

In the name of the Father, the Son, and the Holy Spirit, amen.

MESSterpiece REMINDER:
No matter how broken or burdensome I feel, I am forever God's beloved.

Chapter 4

if i ONLY KNEW THEN

. . . to proclaim freedom for the captives and release from darkness
for the prisoners . . .

Isaiah 61:1

Trigger warning: In this chapter, I discuss losing a loved one. I know this may stir up a myriad of emotions for you, so please be kind and gentle with yourself as we allow grief and sorrow a seat at the table.

IT WAS THE FIRST DAY of July, and the house was quiet as my daughter napped. I was sitting at the table doodling on my computer and feeling the kicks and stretches of the baby boy growing inside me when the phone rang. My sister's name, number, and photo appeared, so I slid my finger across the screen to answer the call. But she did not greet me with her typical silly salutation. All I heard were gasps of breath between the sobs she was trying so hard to suppress. My stomach sank. "What's wrong?" I pleaded. The words that finally crawled across her lips pricked my ears like thorns: "NiNi died last night."

My mind raced. My heart pounded. The tears started falling, and a tidal wave of guilt and regret crashed over me. The last conversation I had with my aunt, whom we affectionately called NiNi, did not reflect the love and dignity we had for each other. Instead, we found ourselves confined by the ropes of our frustrations, contending until the tension between us was as thick as a wall. If only I knew then what I know now.

My aunt had not been herself for a few years. After going through a terrible ordeal with a man we had all grown to know and love, her zest for life slowly began to fade. She moved in with my grandmother, her mom, and secluded herself from the world. When I visited her in Memphis the summer before, I could not wrap my head around seeing my aunt, who had been the spunkiest person I knew, confined to a bed with no plan to improve her situation.

From my point of view, she could come out on top if she would just try. *If* held all my desperate hopes for her. If she would just get out of bed, she would gain some perspective. If she would just go to the doctor, they could help her. If she would just get over the man who had broken her heart, she could put her life back together. Why couldn't she just woman up, take some responsibility, and snap out of it? If only I knew then what I know now.

Our conversation turned into an all-out brawl when the anger brewing under the surface of my fake smile couldn't be tucked away any longer. I put my gloves on and entered the ring to fight against her resolve to lay there and die. I swung the first punch with a passive-aggressive comment about her needing to take responsibility and stop blaming everyone else for her ending up this way. She put her gloves on and punched back with condescension for my disrespect. We duked it out for a while. But when the bell rang, we were both defeated.

I didn't understand the disease of depression and how it debilitated its victims. I just wanted my aunt back. I wanted her to fight. If she wouldn't fight for herself, wouldn't she at least fight to get better for her family? Didn't she love us? Weren't we worth living for?

We hadn't spoken since that awful fight, and now she was gone. This couldn't possibly be how things would end between us. I couldn't comprehend that I'd never get to see or talk to my aunt again. If only I knew then what I know now.

Remembering

NiNi was everything a young girl could hope for in an aunt. She was funny, wise, a little edgy, and always up for an adventure. She had chestnut brown eyes with long lashes that commanded attention. Her hair was a mane of thick black silk, highlighted with silver tresses. Bold color adorned her lips that puckered when she pulled us in for one of her scrumptious smooches. Her heavyset figure never deterred from her ageless beauty. I was in awe of her. She was lovely and likable, with an enthralling vibe that reeled me in, along with all who knew her.

During the drama of my teen years, she was a steady rock I could anchor to. I lived with my grandmother most of my school-aged years and into college. Things would often go sideways, and NiNi was always available with a listening ear or shoulder to cry on. I'd call her when I was ready to pack my bags and run away, and she'd talk me through my feelings and offer me perspective. She'd reminisce about her own childhood and share stories about how funny and winsome Mammaw used to be. She always eased the pain of how hard things had been since Pappaw died. Talking through these tumultuous times with NiNi changed the trajectory of my life. And the thought of never getting a chance to offer back to her some of the life-giving wisdom she once offered me brought me to my knees.

Ultimately NiNi died of a heart attack. But I know now it was the depression that caused her initial decline. If only I knew then what I know now.

Realizing

Our son was born that December. At his baby shower, my grandmother gifted me the blanket she had made for NiNi's nursery. It was pale blue-and-white checkered muslin with petite pink and blue roses on tiny green stems. I lifted it out of the packaging, wrapped it up in my arms, and pulled it close to my heart. Oh, how I wished I were wrapped in her arms instead. Since my son would never get the chance to nuzzle into NiNi's perfume-doused bosom, I did the only other thing I could. I laid his tiny little body onto those soft blue-and-white checkered threads and photographed my newborn son on NiNi's baby blanket—a bittersweet tribute to my aunt who had left us far too soon.

One year later, as I found myself in the throes of depression and generalized anxiety disorder, I would have given anything to be able to call my aunt and tell her, "I understand now. I'm so sorry. You don't have to fight alone." If only I knew then what I know now.

Looking Back to Move Forward

I fell on Janie's gray couch, tortured with grief. My last conversation with NiNi played over and over in my mind. "I wish I knew then what I know now," I declared as hot tears ran down my cheeks.

I was now intimately familiar with depression and how debilitating it could be. And the grief of knowing now what I didn't know then felt suffocating. I would have done it all differently. I would have been proactive in checking in on her. I would have called her when she came to mind. I would have listened to her and loved her through this battle. Instead, I would forever hold the pain of knowing that she died feeling unloved and disrespected . . . by me.

As all my regrets hung thick in the air, making it hard to breathe, Janie asked a very pointed question: "Andrea, are you responsible now for what you didn't know then?"

Her words had to fight their way through a cloud of grief to reach my bewildered mind. I knew the correct answer was, "No, I'm not responsible for what I didn't know," but my heart mourned what I couldn't change or make right. Perhaps you understand that pain too?

Merriam Webster offers two definitions for *regret*: 1) "to mourn the loss of, to miss very much, to be very sorry for;" 2) "sorrow aroused by circumstances beyond one's control or power to repair."[10] In my research on regret, I discovered a deeper work at play. While I was experiencing profound sadness over things outside of my control—like NiNi's death and my lack of knowledge around her disease when I saw her last—I was also experiencing intense guilt for things within my control—like my words, my actions, and my inactions. I now understand that the things outside our control produce regret, while the things within our control produce remorse.[11] Remorse involves personal responsibility. Regret does not.

During my session with Janie that day, she guided me in differentiating what was in my control and what wasn't. I acknowledged my regret for not being able to talk to her again because she died, and I identified my remorse for not being able to ask her forgiveness for the things I said when she was alive. Slowly, through a stream of tears and muddled prayers, I began to forgive myself.

I forgave myself for not having all the answers and for saying the wrong thing at the wrong time. I made peace with the fact that my heart was in the right place, even though my words didn't show it. I released myself for not grasping the severity of the situation, and I came to terms with the fact that even if I had known then what I know now, things may have turned out the same way. I couldn't have saved her. None of us could have.

And I wrote a letter to my aunt expressing all the things I wish I could have said to her. Even though she'd never get the chance to read it, writing out what I wish I could have said helped me further seal the forgiveness I desperately needed to offer myself. Contending with my remorse helped me properly cope with my regrets.

The regrets resurface each year on the anniversary of her death, and I grieve all over again. Grief is, after all, the evidence of how deeply we loved the person we've lost. But the sting of remorse has diminished because of the work I did in learning to forgive myself. I was only able to move forward by looking back on what I so desperately wished I could change and making peace with it. And forward is where freedom lives.

Forgiving Ourselves

Like David in his psalms, we can experience freedom in our mind, body, and soul when we get gut-honest with God and ourselves:

> Oh, what joy for those whose disobedience is forgiven, whose sin is put out of sight! Yes, what joy for those whose record the LORD has cleared of guilt, whose lives are lived in complete honesty! When I refused to confess my sin, my body wasted away, and I groaned all day long. Day and night your hand of discipline was heavy on me. My strength evaporated like water in the summer heat. Finally, I confessed all my sins to you and stopped trying to hide my guilt. I said to myself, "I will confess

my rebellion to the Lord." And you forgave me! All my guilt is gone. (Psalm 32:1–5 NLT)

Isn't it fascinating to see the connection between our physical health and the stress of unforgiveness? Our bodies weaken when we fail to seek and offer forgiveness. Our pursuit of forgiveness for ourselves is critical to our overall health and the well-being of our relationships. But forgiveness can be a challenging process that takes many shapes.

In the next chapter, we'll discuss the arduous process of forgiving someone who has hurt us, even as we remember the pain their offense continues to cause. It can feel unsubstantiated and absurd to forgive someone who has not sought resolution for their actions, but the painful truth is that our unforgiveness toward them keeps us imprisoned while they go free. The same is true when we fail to forgive ourselves. We remain a captive. And until we make peace with ourselves, it will be significantly harder to truly forgive those who have caused us pain.

Feelings of unworthiness and shame can keep us from extending forgiveness to ourselves. But God shows us through David's numerous offenses, including adultery and murder, that when we take ownership of our actions and honestly confess our mistakes and shortcomings to God, He forgives us and wipes our slate clean. Receiving God's forgiveness allows us to forgive others, including ourselves, and release the shame that hinders our growth and joy. Like David, you and I can experience freedom from all our guilt. And in case there is any doubt, *all* translated in the original Hebrew means "all."

So what has your body wasting away? What do you need to forgive yourself for?

Is there something you know now that you didn't know then that is nagging you with regret? Did you do or say something that has you filled with remorse? Perhaps something went unsaid or undone? What conversation would you give anything to do over or have a follow-up? Write down the first thing that comes to mind below.

_____

_____

_____

Allow yourself to be comforted by Jesus right now. He came to "comfort all who mourn and provide for those who grieve in Zion" (Isaiah 61:2–3). That includes you and me. He's not asking you to rush past this uncomfortable feeling. He's inviting you to sit with Him. You can tell Him everything on your mind, or you can cry in silence. There's no right or wrong way to grieve. He welcomes your tears, your words, your rage, your regret, your remorse. There is nothing you can bring in this moment that He's not ready to hold.

Bring it all and allow Him to comfort you. Allow Him to provide everything you need to grieve well. Listen for His voice. Be on the lookout for His provision, especially in unexpected places. And keep coming back to Him. Every time that pain pinches your nerves or stops your breath, come back to Him and let Him comfort you.

Remember, we are not held responsible now for things we didn't know then. The door to that prison cell is already unlocked! But the choice is ours. We can stay locked away, chained to walls of regret, or we can shake off those shackles and walk out in the freedom Jesus offers us.

Not all broken relationships can or should be put back together. But in forgiving ourselves for our part of the damage, we can move forward in freedom—the kind of freedom Jesus offers to all captives longing to be released from the shackles of unforgiveness. By accepting God's forgiveness for our sins, we can then extend mercy and grace to those who have sinned against us.

(RE)FRAME IT

Let's take a moment to identify how our beliefs affect our behavior, which lies need to be replaced with truth, and what steps we can take to move toward whole health.

WORLDVIEW: How has my upbringing affected my mindset?
When did you first learn about forgiveness? Was forgiveness modeled in your home growing up?

BELIEFS: How has my worldview filtered what I believe to be true?
What was your initial understanding of what forgiveness was and what was required to obtain it? Have those beliefs changed or morphed over time?

VALUES: How have my beliefs framed what I value?
Were you taught to own up to your mistakes and ask the person you hurt for forgiveness? Or were you taught to stuff your feelings, save face, and act like everything was fine?

CHOICES: How have my values influenced my choices?
Is forgiveness something you have come to honor and pursue in your own life? Have you ever experienced the value of offering yourself forgiveness for things you did or didn't do that brought pain or harm to others?

RESULT: How have my choices helped or hurt me and those around me?
How has not forgiving yourself for things you regret impacted your life? How could forgiving yourself positively affect your life, decisions, and relationships?

If you're ready to take the brave step toward forgiving yourself today, the exercise below will help guide you through the process.

Before you begin, schedule a time when you'll be uninterrupted and in a safe space where you can allow all your feelings to surface. It's okay to work through this exercise alone or to invite a trusted counselor, coach, pastor, or friend into the process with you. Be gentle with yourself as you reflect honestly on what happened. It's important to only work through one incident at a time. You can use this exercise as many times as you need to handle each specific event of regret and remorse that's holding you from experiencing freedom.

Step 1: Take out a sheet of paper and draw a line down the middle.

Step 2: Recall the situation you listed above (only one at a time if there are multiple occasions). On the left side, write *REGRET* at the top. List out all the pieces of this situation that were outside of your control. Be as specific as possible.

Step 3: On the right side, write *REMORSE* at the top. List out all the things that were inside your control. Be as specific as possible.

Step 4: Once you've distinguished what is regret—things outside of your control—go through each one and declare these words out loud: "I no longer hold myself responsible for what was outside of my control. I no longer take the blame for what I didn't yet know or understand." There is power in declaring things out loud with your own voice.

Step 5: Now move over to the column with the elements of remorse— things you did or didn't say or do that caused pain or harm to another person. For each item that was within your control, declare these words out loud: "I forgive myself for my actions and words that caused me pain then and continue to cause me pain now. I release the feelings of anger and resentment I've harbored toward myself for what happened."

Step 6: If you are able to speak with the person you hurt, set up a time to talk, apologize, and ask them for forgiveness. Use the elements in steps 2 and 3 to help you plan your apology. If you are unable to speak to that person, either because of death or boundaries set in place for safety or health, write a letter outlining everything you would have said to them face to face if you could. Use the elements in steps 2 and 3 to help you create the letter.

PRAY ABOUT IT

Elohay Selichot, you are the God of forgiveness. Thank you for offering forgiveness to me, even though I don't deserve it. There's so much I wish I could go back and redo with the knowledge and insight I have now. But until I let go of this regret, I can't move forward in your freedom. Please help me.

Help me forgive myself for what I did, said, and believed before I understood the complexity of the situation. Help me also forgive myself for what I didn't do or say out of fear, ignorance, or anger. Forgive me for the pain I've caused, whether intentionally or inadvertently. I want to make peace with the past so I can move forward into a restorative future. Thank you for your comfort, strength, and wisdom as I learn to forgive myself and others.

In the name of the Father, the Son, and the Holy Spirit, amen.

MESSterpiece REMINDER:
Knowing now what I didn't know then is so painful, but I'm learning to release myself from the chains of regret and extend forgiveness to myself.

Chapter 5

THE TROUBLE WiTH TRAUMA

*... to proclaim the year of the Lord's favor and
the day of vengeance of our God ...*
Isaiah 61:2

Trigger warning: While no specific trauma will be discussed in detail, the stories in this chapter may trigger unresolved pain in your heart, mind, and body. Be gentle with yourself. Give yourself permission to allow the pendulum of emotions to surface and swing. Consider ways you can prepare ahead of time to hold these emotions in a healthy way. If you need support, please reach out to a trusted friend or counselor. It may also better serve you to come back to this chapter at a later point when you have done more healing.

THE ROOM WAS FILLED WITH our family and friends. Each guest held a cupcake and impatiently awaited the signal to sink their teeth in. The center of one, and only one, delicious pastry would reveal the gender of the little nugget who would give me the title I had longed to hold since I was a little girl ... mom. In one simultaneous surge, everyone took a bite and eagerly surveyed the crowd, but only white cream spilled out. Everyone clamored for me to take another bite. I lifted the cupcake to my lips, pausing for a brief moment in eager anticipation, and shoved another mouthful of vanilla cake into my mouth. I pulled the tasty treat away from my face and a dollop of pink frosting peeked through. The crowd erupted in shouts of joy: "It's a girl!"

Isn't it amazing how a single moment, and the color of icing in a single cupcake, can change a person's life forever?

There are a few momentous moments that are marked with stars on the maps of our lives. Some are beautiful memories we want to remember in detail. Others are painful prisons we yearn to bury and forget forever. Yet we hold them both. Joy and pain are two unlikely friends who hold hands throughout our lives. For me, and maybe for you too, the joy of becoming a mom continues to hold hands with pain from my past. It's hard to move forward when you're constantly being pulled backward.

Next to saying, "I do," becoming a mom was my greatest dream. But now that it was actually happening, I felt plagued with fear that my baggage would cripple my ability to do it well. A person is never truly prepared to become a parent. Heck, I was still figuring out how to be a wife! But life and all its responsibilities keep coming, ready or not.

Our daughter came into the world as bald as her daddy and as sweet as pecan pie. But after having to be induced, I was like a zombie when they placed her in my arms at 3:42 a.m. that August morning. My body had taken quite a beating bringing that precious baby girl into the world, and I was swaying up and down on a seesaw of elated delight and utter exhaustion.

After two days of 24/7 assistance, it was time to go home. And, y'all, I cried. How was I going to survive without that adjustable hospital bed? And the incredible nursing staff to help me do everyday tasks, like peeing on my own? And breastfeeding? And sleeping? I felt severely inadequate to care for myself, much less a completely dependent baby. I still had so much to learn and so many growing edges. *How was I qualified to raise a person? Isn't there some sort of certification I should receive to be eligible for such an important job?*

Nope. They just wheel you out to your car with a few diapers as a parting gift and wish you well on your parenting journey. We were parents—her parents. And it was up to us now to meet our daughter's needs and help her blossom and grow into a healthy, capable person. That role is both empowering and terrifying.

As I laid that sweet, innocent baby girl down for a nap one afternoon, I talked to God about all the things that haunted my imagination. I wanted nothing more than to keep her wrapped in a bubble of protection, safe from all the things that would cause her pain. Safety had become like a religion to me. I put so much hope in it. But God saw through my fear and leaned in toward me instead of pulling away in frustration, as so many others had done throughout my life. He whispered, *Andrea, you can't keep bad things from happening to her. But you can be there to help her heal when they do.*

The knot in my stomach slowly began to unravel, and my racing mind decelerated for a moment while I took this thought in. God wasn't making me a promise that something bad wouldn't happen to her, which is what I really wanted. But He was assuring me that together we would get through whatever the world threw at us, which is what I really needed. This is actually how God has been caring for His kids for generations.

> But now, O Jacob, listen to the LORD who created you. O Israel, the one who formed you says, "Don't be afraid, for I have ransomed you. I have called you by name; you are mine. When you go through deep waters, I will be with you. When you go through rivers of difficulty, you will not drown. When you walk through the fire of oppression, you will not be burned up; the flames will not consume you. For I am the LORD, your God, the Holy One of Israel, your Savior. I gave Egypt as a ransom for your freedom . . . You are honored, and I love you. Do not be afraid, for I am with you." (Isaiah 43:1–5 NLT)

To put this Scripture in context, the Israelites, who were God's chosen people and the descendants of Abraham, had been enslaved by the Babylonian Empire for seventy years. They had abandoned Yahweh, worshiped other gods, and given in to sin and temptation. But in spite of their rebellion, God urges them to remember how deeply He loves them. He reminds them that He is with them—ahead, behind, and beside them—as they endure oppression, trouble, and fear. And just like He did for their ancestors when He led them out of Egypt through the Red Sea, He promises to release them from captivity, guide them safely home, and help them rebuild their nation. He doesn't sugarcoat how hard the journey ahead will be, but He assures them He'll be by their side through all the bumps and bruises.

This resonates in my bones. I, too, have been in captivity. And as a captive to the effects of my sin and the sin of others, I became a worshiper of other gods, like safety, self-preservation, and satisfaction. I, too, have sought things to bring immediate relief instead of waiting on God's deliverance. And I, too, have had the God of the universe walking with me through every deep water and great trouble. Perhaps you, too, know the perplexity of that path.

Not If, but When. Not Why, but How.

As someone who has lived through various traumatic experiences, it's hard to swallow that God says tribulation is a *when*, not an *if* scenario.

It didn't take long after I began meeting with Janie for the pain to surface from an incident of sexual abuse I experienced as a seven-year-old little girl. For so long, I had been asking God, "Why?" *God, if you're so good, why did you allow this to happen to me? Why do you allow such horrible things to happen to innocent people?*

The concept of why a good God allows bad things to happen rattles us to our bones. We need a safe space with a biblically grounded mentor to work through this disorienting dilemma. But I'd like to redirect our attention from what we cannot affect to what we can. When I (re)framed my question from "Why did this happen?" to "How can I heal from what has happened?" I stepped into deeper healing and freedom. I pray you will too.

Forgiving as We Remember

In her book, *Forgiving What You Can't Forget*, Lysa TerKeurst explains that forgiveness is both a decision and a process. It's both/and. When faced with the decision to forgive a trauma, we not only have to look at how our lives were immediately altered by what happened but also how our lives have been repeatedly impacted long-term. She breaks it down this way: "The decision to forgive acknowledges the facts of what happened. But the much longer journey of forgiveness is around all the many ways these facts affected you—the impact they created."[12]

Traumatic offenses are not simply forgiven and forgotten, despite what many of us have been told. Forgiving and forgetting are two distinct concepts. Forgiveness is an extension of the supernatural grace and mercy of God, and it is needed for our own sake and sanity. While Jesus teaches us to "forgive us our debts, as we also have forgiven our debtors" (Matthew 6:12), He does not offer a memory zapper to erase what's happened to us. Instead, we must learn to forgive as we remember. This will be a lifelong process requiring guidance, wisdom, and care.

Trauma victims are painfully familiar with the twofold nature of forgiveness. Even years after the initial offense, our lives are still disrupted in ways that continue to surprise us and catch us off guard. We find ourselves stuck in the tar of remembering what happened while grappling to consider what it could look like to forgive something so unforgivable. The full impact of the trauma is too big to grasp all at once, but the void in our souls is unmistakable.

In my weekly meetings with Janie, it became clear that the unhealed traumas from my childhood were wreaking havoc on my life, mindset, and body. There was deeper work to be done, and it would require every ounce of grit this girl possessed and then some. But I wanted out of this prison cell. So I pushed through my apprehension and signed up for a program my friend, Corinna, recommended—an intensive nine-month course called Life Skills: Learning to Live, Learning to Love.

Life Skills

As an educational organization, the goal of Life Skills International is to help people break free from harmful behavior patterns and build new, healthy foundations for life and relationships. I can't recommend this curriculum enough. But I almost walked out of the first meeting.

I entered a room of fourteen complete strangers and took a seat at the table facing forward. The other fold-out tables faced each other, making a U-shape. We were each handed a stack of papers to read and sign. Since this group dealt with trauma and abuse, it was critical that the things shared in the room stayed in the room. That all made sense, so I squiggled my John Hancock across page after page until one stopped me dead in my tracks.

It was titled "The 100 Percent Rule," and it stated, in no uncertain terms, that I am one hundred percent responsible for my feelings, thoughts, actions, speech, and behavior. It emphasized that other people don't make me feel mad, sad, glad, etcetera, but that I choose to feel, think, speak, and behave the way I do—no matter the influence of those around me.

Excuse me? I'm choosing the way I feel? My abuser is held zero percent accountable for the change in my thoughts, feelings, and subsequent behaviors, while I am held one hundred percent responsible to think, feel, and behave in a way that does not reflect the fact that I've been exploited? My veins ran hot with contempt. A temper tantrum brewed under the surface of my skin as I stared those words down. Surprisingly, my anger was matched by a meddlesome curiosity to hear this offensive claim explained.

I reluctantly signed my name, turned in the pile of papers, and waited for the leader to address the elephant in the room. With a black dry erase marker, she wrote the central theme of the Life Skills program across the whiteboard: "If you are teachable, it is fixable."

I read the words again and again, questioning the scope of their meaning.

If I am teachable, *(then)* it is fixable?

If *I* am teachable, *it* is fixable?

If I *am* teachable, it *is* fixable?

If I am *teachable*, it is *fixable*?

Like the 100 Percent Rule, this theme seemed to put the brunt of the burden on my shoulders, and that seemed so unfair. Internally, I pitched another hissy fit. *What about the people who hurt me? They're just off the hook? It's all up to me to fix this? I'm the one who needs to be teachable?*

Have you felt a similar weight of injustice? Have you cried out to God in anger, bitterness, and confusion? You are not alone. God can handle, and even welcomes, all the feelings that stir within us. He cries with us over the things that happened to us that never should have happened. He also weeps for our abusers. But do not be mistaken—God will bring justice to unrighteousness in His perfect way. Even if we never see justice won here on earth with our own eyes, we can be certain sin will be held accountable before the throne room of our heavenly Judge (Romans 12:19; Revelation 20:11–12).

As we unpacked the benefits of being teachable, I realized I had missed its message of hope. Being teachable and taking responsibility for what was mine, and letting go of what was not, wasn't another weight to bear—it was the key to my freedom. My healing was not in their hands—it was in mine.

Up until this point, I had been waiting around for the people who had hurt me to own up to their mistakes and apologize. As you can imagine and may relate to, this only created more time and opportunities for me to continue down the destructive path my pain had paved. I was stuck in a victim mentality, drinking the poison myself but waiting eagerly for someone else to suffer the consequences.

But now I had a choice before me, with tools to help me take my healing into my own hands. It was going to be work, and it would have to begin with (*gulp*) me taking responsibility for my thoughts, feelings, and actions. But in learning what was mine to hold, I was also going to learn what was not mine to hold. And that would help me move from a victim mentality to a survivor mentality.

Embracing a survivor mindset empowered me to accept the fact that what happened to me was out of my control, but what happens now is within my control. Taking ownership of my healing journey, regardless of my offender's remorse, created the space for me to begin to repair what was broken and rebuild what had been destroyed (Isaiah 61:4).

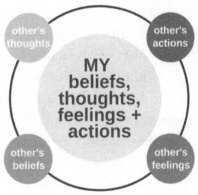

Check-in: How are you doing? I know so much has been stolen from you, but so much can be restored. I pray for hope to trickle into your heart as you read. Take a moment to check in with yourself to see if you need a break or if you're okay to keep going.

Arrested Development

One of the first things we discussed in Life Skills was the concept of *arrested development,* the impact of unresolved trauma on emotional development. Life Skills founder, Dr. Paul Hegstrom, asserts that when an adult has unresolved childhood trauma, particularly rejection, incest, molestation, or emotional and physical abuse, their emotional development will not progress beyond the age they were at the time of the trauma.[13]

Cue: major a-ha moment. This explained why I felt like a seven-year-old walking around in a forty-year-old body! Those of us who have experienced childhood trauma can see the results of arrested development as we look at our self-image and our capacity to thrive, or merely survive, in personal and professional relationships. Fascinating, right? And super frustrating. I had a thirty-year emotional gap to bridge. But how?

The honest answer: slowly, painfully, and intentionally.

I've learned to look at that seven-year-old little girl and have compassion on her. I remember that she still lives inside of me, and I can love her, mentor her, and help her heal. When I notice her cries for help when my trauma resurfaces, I can respond to her gently instead of being frustrated that she's still there. I pray you find the same tenderness for the little girl inside of you who is looking for a safe person to put her trust in.

While the details of our stories are different, we're all figuring out how to deal with the aftermath of what happened to us. We're becoming aware of how our identity, faith, and health have been impacted by the trauma we endured. Perhaps in your story, like mine, you told a trusted adult what happened only to be silenced in disbelief. Instead of wrapping you up in their arms and offering you the love, validation, and support you desperately needed, they may have insisted:

"There's no way that could have happened."

"You must have dreamed it."

"So-and-so would never do such a thing."

But so-and-so did do such a thing. And we never in a million years thought the person who was supposed to care for us in our greatest moment of need would insist we bury our story, keep quiet, and pretend it never happened. So we closed our mouths, but our bodies began to scream out in rebellion with unexplained stomachaches and digestive problems, sensitivity to light and sound, migraines, chronic pain, fatigue, autoimmune disorders, or asthma.[14]

Longing for attention and affection, some of us have become people-pleasing codependents who are unable to decipher our own worth and value outside of the approval and validation of others. Longing for a sense of control, some of us have found ourselves battling addictions to food, drugs, alcohol, work, sex, power, success, or self-harm. Many of us have sought or given in to physical intimacy no matter our values, religious beliefs, or morals. And when we couldn't find it in the arms of another, we've taken care of it ourselves. Our constant desire for arousal and pleasure has left us feeling ashamed, confused, and more alone than ever.

With so many things outside of our control, we've sought after things to give us an immediate high and sense of relief. And for brief moments, we feel better. But what comes up will always come down. So we keep seeking the highs with little to no regard for the damage we've inflicted on ourselves and those around us. PTSD (post-traumatic stress disorder) courses through our veins, and the wounds of not getting the care we needed as children make it hard to function as adults.

If you, like me, have been holding on to these hidden heartaches that have limited your ability to love, be loved, and thrive in healthy ways, know that you are not alone. And just in case no one has ever told you, let me just say: I believe you. I believe you're telling the truth about your story, even if it's unfathomable for someone you love to grasp.

And because you may never hear it from your abuser, let me just say it: I'm sorry. I'm so sorry for what you've endured and for what you may still be enduring. What happened to you is not okay, and you have permission to feel all your feelings about your trauma. You have permission to yell, scream, and cry in order to allow what's inside of you to be released. You also have permission to heal. You do not have to stay stuck here. You can take steps toward freedom. You can embrace the power of Jesus to turn your ashes into beauty, your mourning into joy, and your despair into praise. I'm believing for you. You can heal because the Holy Spirit of God is with you and within you.

One Step at a Time

Being teachable is easier said than done, especially when the pain and complications of past and present trauma blur our eyes to the goodness of God. We can't prevent bad things from happening. Nor can we go back and change the traumas we've already endured. But we can make a choice. We can choose to stop waiting on our abusers to repent and, instead, lean into the many therapeutic resources available to us. We can move from being victims to being survivors. And with the help of Jesus and His community, we can begin to heal what's been broken and walk out of our prison cells into the freedom Jesus offers.

We did not get a choice in what happened to us. But we do get a choice in how we respond to what happened. We can learn to embrace healthy ways of thinking about ourselves and others. We can learn to own what's ours and let go of what's not. And even if we take two steps forward and one step back, we've still taken one step forward. And that is one step toward freedom.

As you continue your journey, let me offer you a script that continues to help me put one foot in front of the other as I strive to forgive as I remember:

- I didn't choose what happened to me. But I choose to allow my mind, body, and spirit to heal now.
- I accept the feelings of _____ that are surfacing as I remember what happened.
- I choose to love myself and accept God's love for me right now, just as I am.
- I choose to forgive _____ for _____.
- Forgiving as I remember allows me to be set free.

May it be so.

(RE)FRAME IT

Let's take a moment to identify how our beliefs affect our behavior, which lies need to be replaced with truth, and what steps we can take to move toward whole health.

WORLDVIEW: How has my upbringing affected my mindset?
How were difficult subjects handled in your home growing up? Were you taught to openly discuss them? Or was it not acceptable to bring uncomfortable issues to the table?

BELIEFS: How has my worldview filtered what I believe to be true?
Were you taught to take responsibility for your actions or to blame others?

VALUES: How have my beliefs framed what I value?
Which was held in higher regard in your family growing up: character or reputation? What did you come to believe about your emotions? Good, bad, acceptable, unacceptable, etc.? Were certain emotions praised while others were punished? How did these values impact your ability to heal from trauma?

CHOICES: How have my values influenced my choices?
What coping techniques have you adopted, whether good or bad, based on the values above?

RESULT: How have my choices helped or hurt me and those around me?
What role has God, the Bible, church, and/or biblical counsel played in your healing journey?

If you've been hurt by people who were supposed to help you, would you be willing to try again? Would you consider sitting down with another person/pastor/counselor/therapist to guide you toward the freedom that Jesus is offering you? If someone you trust has a resource they trust, you are likely to find a safe space to begin healing. You may not find the right person on the first try, so don't get discouraged if it takes some time. Be very gentle and gracious with yourself.

Here are some potential actions steps to take today:

- Research therapists in your area or online at https://www.betterhelp.com/.
- Ask a friend for the name of a coach, counselor, or program they recommend.
- Find a Life Skills International class near you at https://www.lifeskillsintl.org/.
- Email or call your church and/or doctor's office to see what resources are available.

PRAY ABOUT iT

Jehovah Ezrah, you are the Lord, my helper. I'm ready to break the shackles of unforgiveness and practice forgiving my offender(s) even as I remember their crimes against me. But I can't do this without your help.

You know about my trauma and the help I need to heal. You know the scripts that need to be rewritten and the spaces I'm stuck. My body has kept score and remembers each offense in detail. I invite you into the dismal abyss where my pain lives and grows.

Guide me to biblically grounded counselors and trained professionals who can support me on this journey. Give me wisdom and grace as I learn how to take responsibility for my thoughts, feelings, and behavior—even though my scars will be part of my story. Help me embrace a survivor mindset by taking ownership of what happens next. I'm done waiting on the people who hurt me to own up to their mistakes. I'm ready to move forward today. Thank you for helping me put one foot in front of the other as I learn to walk in your freedom.

In the name of the Father, the Son, and the Holy Spirit, amen.

MESSterpiece REMINDER

Forgiveness is both a decision and a process, and I'm learning to forgive as I remember.

Chapter 6

MEDICATION: FRIEND OR FOE?

. . . to comfort all who mourn, and provide for those who grieve in Zion—
Isaiah 61:2–3

Trigger warning: If you've dealt with anxiety or depression, chances are high you've had thoughts that those you love would be better off without you. I just want to give you a heads up that I discuss those feelings in this chapter. Remember, you are not alone if you're struggling.

I SAT ON THE GRAY couch across from Janie, as I had done every Thursday that year. A large throw pillow lay ready to ease the hopelessness that filled the air. My countless attempts to treat my anxiety and depression with natural remedies had fallen short, and just thinking about the side effects of antidepressant medications sent me into a panic. I mean, have you seen those commercials with their endless list of risks and dangerous reactions? And the pot of gold at the end of that rainbow? You guessed it—risk of suicide. Great.

My mind was already plagued with suicide ideations. I had a faithful husband, a one-year-old son, and a three-year-old daughter, but all I could think was how much better off they'd be without me. I felt like a raging tsunami, bringing disaster upon everything I touched. And I was certain my mess was messing everything up for them. I didn't have a plan to end my life. But I did imagine how much better my family's life would be if

I was out of the picture. I didn't want to hurt myself, but if I died in a car accident, at least then my family could move on with their lives, free of the burdens I caused them. (I now know this is referred to as passive suicide ideation versus active suicide ideation.)

For months, I prayed for God to take the pain away. To make it stop. To do a miracle. All it would take was the snap of His finger or a word from His lips, and boom. It's done. It's gone. It's healed. But my pleas to God for help seemed to fall on deaf ears. I began to question everything because nothing made sense anymore. I began to doubt . . . not in what God could do for me but in what God would do for me. No amount of trust, prayers, or faith was slowing my steady decline into despair. Nothing was working, and I was running out of hope that things could ever get better.

So here we were again, Janie and I, treading the waters of *what if?*

What If?

The topic of medication had come up several times in my sessions with Janie. And she was in no way twisting my arm to go on medication. It's just that she was able to see the potential benefits of how it could help me. Meanwhile, all I saw was the endless list of what could go wrong: *What if the medication makes things worse?* (Remember, I had already lived through the nightmare of migraine meds and knew how miserable side effects could be.) *What if instead of just imagining that my family would be better off without me I felt compelled to make a plan to end my life? What if I just haven't found the right herbal remedy, essential oil, or diet yet?* 'Cuz it would be more "Christian" for me to utilize something already found in nature, right? #badtheology

Session after session, Janie attentively listened as I drudged up my list of fears. I was ready to throw my hands up in defeat, but she kept leaning in. One afternoon, Janie suggested we look at things from a different angle. Her words that day not only helped me (re)frame my stance on medication but also my outlook on a number of issues in my marriage, motherhood, and ministry. "Andrea, we've spent a lot of time considering what could go wrong. Let's spend some time today considering what could go right."

My breath stopped short in my chest. I heard her words in my ears, yes. But I also felt them flood my heart with hope—hope that had been long buried under despair. And for the first time, there was room in my soul to consider what could go right. *What if this works? What if this helps me get my life back? What if this is God's answer to my pleas for help all along?*

Oh, what freedom a shift in perspective can offer. My view had been so clouded with worst-case scenarios that I was blind to the possibilities of how God could use this painful moment to work something out for my good. It's taken many reluctant years, but I can see now that the seeds planted in hardship can produce some of the richest fruit. The apostle Paul summarized this well in Romans 5:3–5 (NLT):

> We can rejoice, too, when we run into problems and trials, for we know they help us develop endurance. And endurance develops strength of character, and character strengthens our confident hope of salvation. And this hope will not lead to disappointment. For we know how dearly God loves us, because he has given us the Holy Spirit to fill our hearts with his love.

Paul was intimately familiar with hardship, which was crucial for me in his credibility to speak into the vulnerable space of my agony. But instead of promising a quick fix, which is what I wanted, Paul laid out a roadmap of the powerful potential our current pain can produce if we lean into the process.

I had been disappointed and hopeless for so long that I didn't recognize that God was answering my prayers by pointing me back to the very thing I was terrified to try. He knew medication would offer relief to my afflicted brain. He also knew I'd have a tough time adjusting to this idea, so he sent me a profoundly patient therapist. With a (re)framed perspective, my what-if questions began to sound a little different: *What if God does love me that dearly? What if medication is a gift from God to help clear the fog of fear and sadness so I can better endure this dark and difficult season? What if the side effects of what could go right outweigh the side effects of what could go wrong?*

It turns out, for me, they did.

Within the first week, I began to feel long-awaited relief from suicide ideations and fight-or-flight fatigue. I no longer felt like everyone hated me. I no longer wanted to die. And I began to notice my ability to apply the tools I was learning in therapy to my day-to-day life—tools like emotional intelligence, mindfulness, boundaries, and assertiveness. My family and friends began commenting on the positive changes they were seeing, and that put wind beneath my broken wings. This was the *what-could-go-right alternative* Janie was talking about. Thank God for her.

And thank God for the medication. It brought me out of the fog of fear and sadness, and it continues to help me cope with the ongoing symptoms of anxiety and depression. And I'm eternally grateful for that. Medication did not, however, come free of its fair share of less-than-desirable side effects. Some good gifts come with a warning label.

A Note on Side Effects

In a six-year period, I went through eight different medications, trying to find the right brand and dose. Eight. And that process included a couple of trips to the ER, because we found out my body is very sensitive to medication. Side effects have included hair loss, low libido, heart palpitations, acne, migraines, and weight gain.

The truth is, I have a love/hate relationship with these pills. Some days I wish my body would just do what it needs to do so I can be free of these side effects. But I remember what my life was like before medication, and I pause to thank God for His provision, even though it's come in ways that still leave me perplexed.

Some of us will only need medication for a brief time before things balance out chemically. Others of us will have to swallow that little pill every day for the rest of our lives. And still some will not benefit from or be able to tolerate medication. Your journey will be unique to you if you decide to give medication a try to help clear the fog and help you function.

TIP: It's important, especially when beginning a new medication or weaning off of one, to keep track of your symptoms. I recommend keeping a weekly planner by your bed to easily track your daily progress and symptoms. Just take a few minutes at the end of each day to write down how you're feeling and note any side effects, both good and bad, you experienced that day. This will prove tremendously helpful, not only for your own sake but also in conversations with your doctor.

Shattering Stigmas

Our faith in Christ and the power of the Holy Spirit are not marred by our need for professional or medical help. I believe reaching out for help is practicing the God-given art of wisdom. And wisdom leads to discernment: "If you need wisdom, ask our generous God, and He will give it to you. He will not rebuke you for asking" (James 1:5 NLT).

Not for a moment do I believe God designed and gifted people with the capacity to endure such professions as doctors, nurses, scientists, therapists, and counselors only to disapprove of our reaching out for their expertise when we are ill, struggling, or in need of direction. Jesus is the only source of true hope. But anxiety and depression can blur our eyes and blind our hearts to His goodness. So He uses His divinely crafted creation as His hands and feet in this broken world to help us grasp His hope.

For so long, I believed I was suffering because I just didn't have enough faith. But in reality, I was suffering because my brain was sick. And that was affecting every area of my life physically, mentally, emotionally, and spiritually. I firmly believe that God worked through Janie to help me discern that I first needed to address the physical/chemical piece of the puzzle before I could address the mental, emotional, and spiritual facets that also needed attention. My faith was being drowned by fear and shame, and God knew that medication would stabilize my brain so I could once again grasp reality and the truth of His unwavering love for me—even in the midst of mental illness.

God didn't promise to make all our problems disappear when we put our trust in Jesus, but He did promise to be with us as we face the joys and uncertainties each day brings. When we turn to Him for help for our anxiety and depression, He may tell us to pick up the phone and call the doctor, sign up for that class through the hospital, make that appointment to speak to a therapist, or give that medication a try.

Jesus came to bind up our broken hearts, to free us from the captivity of shame and stigmas, and to release us from the prisons of our minds and the hopelessness of failing health. You may be in a season where fear and sadness are calling the shots in your mind and body, but hope and healing are still yours for the taking. Keep reaching out for the support of friends and family. And keep turning to Jesus for wisdom and discernment. He will make a path for you.

May you be free from the shackles of shame and stigmas as you seek God for wisdom.

(RE)FRAME IT

Let's take a moment to identify how our beliefs affect our behavior, which lies need to be replaced with truth, and what steps we can take to move toward whole health.

WORLDVIEW: How has my upbringing affected my mindset?
How was invisible illness, whether mental, emotional, or physical, handled in your home growing up? Did you have a safe person to talk to about your pain, or were you told it was all in your head? What was the general view on medication in your home growing up?

BELIEFS: How has my worldview filtered what I believe to be true?
As a Christian, were you taught to believe that loving Jesus would make your life easier and shield you from experiencing the pain of this world? How has this belief impacted you? What did you come to believe to be true about medications for mental health as a result of the worldview of your caregivers and people of influence?

VALUES: How have my beliefs framed what I value?
Do you struggle with shame and fear around the issue of medication for anxiety and depression?

CHOICES: How have my values influenced my choices?

How have you behaved in response to the worldview, beliefs, and values around health and faith? Have you shied away from things out of fear? Pushed yourself to your physical limits to prove your worth? Succumbed to shame and punished your body because you were convinced your poor physical and mental health meant God was mad or disappointed in you for not having enough faith? Do you sense God asking you to shift your mindset around medication, either for yourself or for someone you know and love?

 RESULT: How have my choices helped or hurt me and those around me?

If worst-case scenarios are clouding your view today, ask God to replace your fear of what could go wrong with the hope of what could go right. What does this shift in perspective feel like for you?

PRAY ABOUT IT

El-Deah, you are the God of knowledge and wisdom. I need your wisdom now. Things have felt hopeless for a while. I'm starting to wonder if things will ever get better. I'm afraid. I'm worried about the many things that could go wrong if I were to give medication a try. Please open my eyes to what you want me to see. If my fear is blocking my healing, please help me consider that the very thing I'm afraid of may be the very thing that will open the door to my prison cell.

You came to set the captives free. I am a captive to fear, and I want to be set free. Free from fear. Free from stigmas. Free from hopelessness. If medication can help me, give me the mindset to consider what could go right. Lead me in your wisdom, Lord.

Guide me to the people who can help me with this process, to the people you have crafted and ordained for this good work. Remove any fear or misconceptions that would keep me from pursuing something that could help clear the fog of fear and sadness so I can better and more fully grasp your unconditional love for me.

In the name of the Father, the Son, and the Holy Spirit, amen.

MESSterpiece REMINDER:
I can love Jesus and take medication. My need for medical help does not lessen my love for or faith in Jesus.

Chapter 7

TOO MUCH AND NOT ENOUGH

. . . to bestow on them a crown of beauty instead of ashes, the oil of joy instead of mourning, and a garment of praise instead of a spirit of despair.

Isaiah 61:3

SPRINGTIME HOLDS THE JOY OF growth and new possibilities for the world. For the students of Riverdale Elementary, spring also held the highlight event of the year—the annual talent show. Okay, maybe this wasn't an unrivaled affair for every student at the school. But for me, it was a night when stars could shine and the dreams I wished for could come true.

Every year since the fourth grade, I prepared a vocal melody to perform. And every year, my big Italian family filled the rows of fold-out metal chairs to cheer me on. The spring of 1996, my eighth-grade year, was no different. The talent ranged from glitzy showmen singing Sinatra to martial arts ninjas to piano prodigies. I watched classmate after classmate show off their skills and bring their A-game to the stage. My act was the final act of the evening, and I would be singing Vanessa Williams's "Save the Best for Last." The irony is only now upon me.

The competitors lined up across the stage, eager to know if they had wowed the judges. First, second, and third place winners were announced in each category, and when they handed me the blue ribbon for first place in the vocal category, I was beside myself with glee. And then, as if in a dream, I heard, "In first place overall for her beautiful performance of 'Save the Best for Last,' Andrea Coletta!" Wait, that's me! They handed me a trophy that was half as tall as my five foot, six inch frame and congratulated me on being automatically qualified to compete in the Mid-South Fair Youth Talent Competition that fall.

Y'all, this was the big leagues. They may as well have just crowned me Miss America!

Hailing from Memphis, Tennessee, the soul capital of the world, I knew exactly which song I wanted to bring to the stage. A blank cassette tape sat ready in my boombox, and I waited eagerly for "Black Velvet" by Alannah Myles to play on the radio. When that unmistakable bluesy guitar riff came through the speakers, my right index finger hit that red record button as fast as lightning. The full-length mirror that hung on my wall endured every practice session of that song over the next four months.

Summer melted into fall, and the big day arrived at my doorstep with crisp September splendor. I wore a long black sequined dress, with a slit from my ankle to my right knee. Half a can of Rave and a hundred bobby pins held my strawberry blonde curls in place. As I stood in the doorway preparing to meet the other big fish from our respective small ponds, I wondered if this self-taught sensation would be able to hold her own against the professionally coached competition.

"Don't worry, you're not going to win anyway," my grandmother asserted as we headed out the door. The click of my high heeled shoes halted against the red brick stone of our entryway, and I froze in stunned disbelief. *What? Why would she say something like that as we're literally walking out the door to my competition?*

Reverse psychology was famous to her generation, and she likely thought her comment would drudge up a high dose of adrenaline that would inspire me to put on the best show of my life and win the whole thing, just like I had done before. But my tender, twelve-year-old heart sank within my chest. And a fear that had just begun to sprout took deep root in my mind that day: *I'm good, but I'm not good enough.*

Out of thirty-six acts, I took ninth place both that year and the following year. The top eight moved on to the next round. And the rest of us were sent home with honorable mentions and shattered dreams. I was one spot away from qualifying. One spot shy of fulfilling my deepest longing. One spot short of proving I was meant to do this.

Good. But not good enough.

Peaches and Coconuts

I first heard the *peach versus coconut metaphor*[15] in my early twenties during a seminary course discussing cross-cultural communication. Unlike the coconut, with its rough exterior layer of protection, peaches are delicate and bruise easily. Coconuts tend to be reserved, slow to trust, and unhurried to break down walls to build new relationships. Peaches tend to be friendly, quick to let their guard down, and eager to make meaningful connections.

After adhering to the reality that I was a fragile fruit living in a callous world, I espoused the term "tender peach" when either describing or defending myself to others. As an adult who's done lots of therapy for my many deep-seated identity issues, I now embrace this term with sincere contentment. But twelve-year-old Andrea did not understand how to balance being a sensitive swan living among quick-witted quail. I always felt a little out of place and got the impression that it was bad or weak to be sensitive and emotional.

Throw-away comments became the record that played on repeat in my mind, insisting I was either too much or not enough:

"You're so gullible."

"It was just a joke. Lighten up."

"Well, someone's got her panties in a twist."

"Stop taking everything so seriously."

"Make up your mind already, we don't have all day."

How about you? What messages did you hear growing up that have shaped how you feel about yourself?

_____

_____

_____

_____

The Risk of Rejection

The thing about peaches and coconuts is that they both run the risk of rejection. Whether we're soft-shelled or thick-skinned, at our core we want to be loved and accepted just as we are. But the opinions and actions of others can leave the impression that we're either too much or not enough. And without realizing it, we begin to form what we believe to be true about ourselves based on what we think others believe about us. Those beliefs profoundly impact our life and relationships.

In her blog post "The Rejection Infection," Lysa TerKeurst recounts a painful memory of being made fun of by some girls at school. The feeling of embarrassment and shame is palpable as she recalls the sound of their laughter at the expense of her self-esteem. Even years later, those feelings of hurt and rejection still impact her: "You can take the girl out of middle school, but for many of us, you can't take the middle school out of the girl."[16]

I felt this . . . deep in my bones.

When I was in middle school, my family couldn't afford to shop at the hip stores at the mall, so I sported previously owned items from Goodwill and the Jaclyn Smith collection from Kmart. Fifth grade girls could be hip and have hips, but you couldn't be curvy and wear knock-off brands. Falling into the latter category, I became the target of mockery for the popular girls in my class. I can't remember all the mean things they said, but I'll remember the hurt I felt for the rest of my life.

Since I had been denied care in my early childhood trauma, all subsequent rejections—from mean girls to bad boyfriends—left that much deeper of a mark on my identity. The fear of someone not liking me or what I brought to the table was always at the center of my mind. I constantly bent over backward to do things *just so* in order to win people's approval. In hopes of making people like me, I took responsibility for things that weren't my fault. I overapologized and overexplained myself, not realizing this was actually making things worse for me.

I struggled in personal relationships. Desperate to hold on to any positive attention I received, I inadvertently pushed people away. My all-consuming dependency on them to make me happy, along with my discontent when they didn't meet my lofty expectations, suffocated the joy out of my relationships. *I was too much.*

Professionally, I doubted my capabilities and waited for permission and praise before feeling any ounce of confidence to move forward on a project. I was timid and rarely took initiative for fear of being shut down. My gregarious and caring personality kept me afloat, but I fell short of my employers' expectations time and again. *I was not enough.*

All too often, instead of looking to Jesus as my source of truth to help me (re)frame my fears and insecurities, I look at those around me to see how I measure up. Instead of seeking affirmation from my Heavenly Father, I seek praise from people as the mark of my success. The comparison trap constantly reels out its dangly carrot, tempting me to take a bite of its deception. Too weak to walk away, I take the bait and sink my teeth into the lie that who I am and what I have is not good enough. The bitter aftertaste lingers, tainting the sweetness of my actual reality.

Did God Really Say . . .?

We've been falling into the traps of the Enemy since the very beginning. Genesis 3 recounts the story most commonly referred to as "The Fall." I would name it, "The One Where Adam and Eve Forgot Who They Were and Whose They Were."

Adam and Eve had everything they could need or want in the garden of Eden. Most notably was the walking, talking presence of the Creator God right there with them. They were living the good life—the perfect life actually. They were free to enjoy every exquisite, nourishing, delicious gift the garden had to offer minus the fruit of one tree at the center of the garden (Genesis 2:16). They gladly abided by God's request to leave that fruit alone until a sneaky serpent asked them a seemingly innocent question: "Did God really say . . .?" (Genesis 3:1).

Perhaps it was because they had never known anything outside of God's perfect love and provision that they couldn't grasp the dire consequences of doubting His words. Nonetheless, the carrot was dangled, and it looked so delicious, so shiny, and so good. "Surely we won't die from eating this," they concluded. So Eve sunk her teeth into the forbidden fruit, and then she gave some to her husband. And their eyes were opened to what life outside of God's perfect truth felt like . . . too much to bear and not enough to make right.

They had been hoodwinked. Four little words strung together planted doubt in the hearts and minds of the image bearers of the Almighty: "Did God really say . . .?"

Yes, God really did say they would die from eating the fruit. They just didn't know it wouldn't be physical death. Instead, and much worse, it would be the death of their perfect relationship. The death of their ability to be naked and unashamed. The death of being shielded from the destruction of sin.

God wasn't holding out on them. He wasn't keeping good things from them. He wasn't hoarding all the best things for Himself. He was protecting them from the lie that His provision was not good enough. He was guarding them against the desire to gain more when they already had all they would ever need. He was being a good Father and asking them to stay away from the one thing that would poison everything.

The understanding of both good and evil is a both/and scenario God never wanted us to embrace. He knew the pain sin would cause and the distance it would create. God is holy and perfect, and holiness and sin simply cannot coexist. The thing is, in order for there to be true love there must be free will. God gave humankind the power to make their own choices with a full understanding that sin could enter their perfect reality and create a chasm that would separate the Father from His beloved image bearers.

The dangling fruit tempts us time and again to doubt God's goodness and His love for us. We reach for the bait, thinking it will make us smarter, stronger, skinnier, more successful, or at a minimum, seen. But one bite is never enough. It never satisfies our craving for love and acceptance. The forbidden fruit will continue to tempt us, so we have to do the proactive work of anchoring our hearts and minds in God's truth. Then, when we're faced with the serpent's sneaky suggestions, we can confidently walk away leaving the bait untouched.

Beliefs and Identity

God wants our identity to be rooted in His unchanging love for us. He knows that who we believe we are impacts how we behave toward others, ourselves, and Him. Our roots affect our fruit. When we believe we're a no good, incapable failure, how we think, speak, and act will inevitably produce the unhealthy fruit of sin, shame, and fear. The trauma, neglect, careless words, thoughtless actions, injustice, and hate of our past spills over into our present, and we find ourselves doing and saying the very things we vowed we never would. Next thing you know, we're placing the root of who we are in what we do.

If this were an Olympic sport, I'd take home the gold every time.

This is why Jesus urges us to stay close to Him: "Remain in me, and I will remain in you. For a branch cannot produce fruit if it is severed from the vine, and you cannot be fruitful unless you remain in me" (John 15:4 NLT).

Jesus invites us to remain in Him because He understands the crucial nutrients we need to survive. Apart from Him, we are brittle and easily wounded. But connected to Him, we are nourished to sustain even the fiercest storms. Connected to Him, we have the capacity to be renewed again and again—as many times as it takes for us to grasp His immeasurable love. This is such good news. It's the truth I need to cling to, particularly as a wife, mom, and leader.

The Slippery Slope of Shame

I make a lot of mistakes. It's just part of being human. And I know now that the healthy way of making amends with those in the wake of my missteps is to own up to my part, apologize, and work toward changing my behavior in the future. The guilt of causing another person harm or discomfort is a powerful gift that helps us restore relationships. But I didn't always follow this framework.

Instead of just feeling bad about what I had done, I would enter a shame spiral in which I convinced myself that I was a terrible, awful, despicable human being who was unworthy of love. Perhaps you know what I'm talking about? I've seen the distinguishment between guilt and shame put this way: Guilt = I did something bad. Shame = I am bad.

In her book *The Gifts of Imperfection,* Brené Brown talks extensively about the damage shame creates in our body, mind, and soul: "Shame is the intensely painful feeling or experience of believing that we are flawed and therefore unworthy of love and belonging."[17] Not limited to only those who've experienced trauma, Brown believes shame is a human condition—something everyone experiences yet also something everyone is afraid to talk about. The good news, she claims, is that if we all have shame, we all have the capacity to build shame resilience. "If we want to live fully, without the constant fear of not being enough, we have to own our story."[18]

Owning my story began with understanding that I'm not responsible for how other people feel about me.

How People Feel About Me

In a therapy session with Janie, I recounted having bumped into a woman I had fallen out of friendship with. She and I had been close, and then one day, she said she needed to pull back. I did my typical, "Oh, sure, yeah, no problem. I totally understand." But the truth was, I didn't understand. And as the weeks passed and she kept her distance, I replayed every conversation, ultimately convincing myself it wasn't something I had done . . . it was me. I was bad. I was unlovable. I was unworthy. Shame.

When I bumped into her a couple of years later, I went into full on people-pleasing mode. I wanted to say all the right things, avoid saying the wrong things, and prove I was worthy of her friendship. As I recalled the encounter, Janie inserted a sobering question that halted my ramblings: "Andrea, are you responsible for how people feel about you?"

My initial instinct was: "Yes! Of course, I am!" I had dedicated endless amounts of mental energy calculating how people felt about me and adjusting myself accordingly. But the longer I sat there, looking into the caring and nonjudgmental eyes of my therapist, a lightbulb went off. *No. I'm really not responsible for how people feel about me!*

Janie helped me understand that what is too much for one person is just right for the next. Not everyone is going to like me. Nor is everyone going to hate me. We each process information, tone, and body language through a unique filter. The experiences we walk into the room with have a profound impact on our interactions with others. The most generous assumption we can make, since we are so keen to make them, is that every person in the room is insecure about something. Every one of us is carrying a burden, past or present, that impacts how we feel about the people around us. These feelings have much more to do with our story than with their personality, mannerisms, or general presence.

(Re)framing my mindset and embracing that I'm not responsible for how other people feel about me flung open the doors to my freedom from shame. And the doors to that prison cell opened at a time when I would need this truth more than ever.

Standing Up to Lead

Frozen with fear, I sat silent for months when I first felt God calling me into a leadership position with the MOPS group at my church. I was convinced that if I raised my hand, I'd be rejected. For so long, my worth had been intertwined with what others thought of me, or at least what I thought they thought of me ('cuz my superpower is mind reading).

I jumped to all the logical conclusions the team was sure to make if they saw my name up for consideration as the new leader of our 100+ woman group:

"Andrea, you're really nice, but we just don't think you're the right fit for this role."

"We really need someone who won't get her feelings hurt so easily."

"This role needs someone strong and confident. You're just too tender and fragile."

I was 100 percent convinced someone else could do it better. So why would God be nudging me to volunteer? Well, the answer to that question became crystal clear: God was digging up the lies I had long believed about myself and restoring my true identity in Him. To Him, I was not only good, but I was very good (Genesis 1). Not only was I very good, but I was also beloved and chosen.

I'm not sure I ever told anyone this, but when I first started coming to MOPS when my daughter was a newborn, I looked at the woman leading that group and thought to myself: *Wouldn't it be something if one day that could be me?* The desire to be a leader was already budding within me— even when I felt like the most unqualified candidate. God planted a seed of hope in my heart that day that would grow through the most tumultuous circumstances and bloom at the most unexpected time.

Qualified or not, God made me to be a leader. And He's called me to be an example of how He makes broken things beautiful again. I've heard it said that "God doesn't call the qualified, He qualifies the called." Had I not followed through on God's nudge to step into a leadership role, I would have missed an important opportunity for Him to show me how much I had healed and how far I had come. It wasn't until I stood up to lead that I realized I had begun standing up to fear and shame and reclaiming my true identity . . . not only good but very good.

All these years later, God still reminds me of His faithfulness. He saw me then and He sees me now. He continues to remind me that because of whose I am, who I am is good. He made me with His holy hands. His Imago Dei (the image of God) flows through me, and His breath of life sustains me. He is a God who exchanges our need to please and our self-sabotage for unconditional love.

Pastor and theologian Timothy Keller sums this up so beautifully: "To be loved but not known is comforting but superficial. To be known and not loved is our greatest fear. But to be fully known and truly loved is, well, a lot like being loved by God. It is what we need more than anything. It liberates us from pretense, humbles us out of our self-righteousness, and fortifies us for any difficulty life can throw at us."[19]

Whatever you're going through, God can use it. He will exchange your ashes for beauty, your grief for joy, and your despair for praise. I pray today that you will practice replacing the fear that you're *too much* and *not enough* with the freedom that you are the *beloved* and *chosen* child of

God. He formed you with His own hands, so you are not only good—you are *very* good.

(RE)FRAME iT

Let's take a moment to identify how our beliefs affect our behavior, which lies need to be replaced with truth, and what steps we can take to move toward whole health.

 WORLDVIEW: How has my upbringing affected my mindset?
What is your earliest memory of believing something (good or bad) was true about you?

BELIEFS: How has my worldview filtered what I believe to be true?
What experiences in your life helped this belief take root as truth?

VALUES: How have my beliefs framed what I value?
How did/does this belief affect your relationship with your family, friends, coworkers, and God? Do you notice a propensity to please? A strong desire to compete and win? The need to always be in control? Do you seek out comfort and security above all else?

CHOICES: How have my values influenced my choices?
What behaviors did/do you adopt because of these values?

RESULT: How have my choices helped or hurt me and those around me?
Does what you've been believing about yourself align with what God says is true about you in Scripture? What step will you take today to help you replace the lie that you're too much and not enough with the truth that you are the beloved, chosen masterpiece of God?

PRAY ABOUT IT

Yahweh-Nissi, you are the Lord, my banner. When the Enemy attacks my identity and makes me question who I am and whose I am, you offer a banner of protection over me. But so often, I forget to stand under it. I've become so vulnerable to the opinions of others and the traps of the Enemy. I have let rejection and shame tell me I'm too much and not enough. But you say I'm not only good but very good. Oh, Lord, help me believe that. I wrap myself in the banner of your protection now and ask you to help me live under the names *beloved* and *chosen*.

Please grow my faith in you and help me stay connected to you. You designed me with the capacity to be renewed again and again, as many times as it takes for me to grasp your immeasurable love. Thank you for that. You know everything about me, all my failures and flaws, and yet your love for me never runs out. That truly is incredible.

Thank you for bending down to give me a garment of praise instead of a spirit of despair.

In the name of the Father, the Son, and the Holy Spirit, amen.

MESSterpiece REMINDER:

I'm learning to let go of feeling responsible for what other people think of me and rest in what God says about me instead.

Chapter 8

BAD MOM

They will be called oaks of righteousness, a planting of the Lord for the display of his splendor. They will rebuild the ancient ruins and restore the places long devastated; they will renew the cities that have been devastated for generations.

Isaiah 61:3–4

IF I'M BEING BRUTALLY HONEST, some days I just want to get in my car, start driving, and not look back. I yearn for the freedom to do whatever I want, whenever I want to do it. I crave the independence of not having to answer to or take care of anyone but myself. I long for open space to spread my wings and fly without wondering how much it will cost or if childcare is provided. I taste the bitterness of marriage and motherhood being so much harder than I ever thought possible, and I despise the envy that courses through my veins and hoodwinks me into believing that everyone else has it better and is doing it better than me. Some days, it's just too much, and I don't feel like I have what it takes to keep up.

There's a disconnect between who I am and who I want to be, a tension between where I shine and where I shatter, a restlessness with feeling like the old me when the new me should be shining through:

- I want to be a good wife, but I have trust issues that threaten the health of my marriage.
- I want to be a good mom, but I have an anger problem that poisons my disposition.

- I want to be a good leader, a faithful disciple of Christ, an oak of righteousness, but I feel stuck and insecure.

Do you know the tension I'm talking about? Whether you're a mom wrangling young kids, a business executive wrangling big deals, or an up-and-coming employee wrangling the endurance to keep stamping that timecard, I bet you know what it's like to have your insecurities and traumas cue a vicious cycle of corruption that can leave you feeling more like a spectacle of sin rather than "a display of the Lord's splendor" (Isaiah 61:4).

These feelings can lead me to depression quicker than you can blink your eyes and fill me with anxiety faster than you can fry an egg on a sidewalk in the scorching summer heat. They're like a prison guard that mocks me by dangling the keys to my freedom just out of reach. Even though Jesus has set me free, I keep ending up behind these bars! How? Why? Because I have an Enemy. And so do you. As we saw in the last chapter, our Enemy is really good at twisting things up in our heads so that we begin to doubt God's goodness and our power and significance as His creation.

The Worst Thing That Could Happen

Remember my epic mom-of-the-year meltdown from chapter two? The one where I screamed at the top of my lungs to my one and three-year-old, "I just can't take this anymore!" Well, let's just say I felt like a complete and utter failure when I walked into therapy that week. I fell on Janie's gray couch and confessed, through tears, "My kids are going to end up in therapy because of me! I'm such a bad mom!"

Messing up my kids felt like the inevitable outcome of my brokenness, and it was my biggest fear. I knew firsthand how the pain of a caregiver can alter the life of a child. After all, hurting people hurt people. And I already felt like I had permanently ruined my kids' lives before they were even in kindergarten. Thankfully, I had a wise counselor with a keen sense of timing. After allowing my fears to linger for a moment, she leaned in and asked, "Andrea, is that the worst thing that could happen to them?"

Whoa.

Her words hung in the air as I grappled with my thoughts.

Would my kids ending up in therapy be the worst thing that could happen to them? My initial instinct was: *Yes, that would be the worst thing because it would prove their brokenness is all my fault!* But as I felt the weight of my body sitting on the couch in the safe space of my therapist's office, I contended with the reality of the situation. *If my kids ended up in therapy, would that be a bad thing? Or would it be an unlikely gift, like it had been for me?*

Little by little, the consequences of the mistakes I was sure to make as a parent, and as a person, felt less and less severe. Janie reminded me that my kids would face pain in their lives that had absolutely nothing to do with me. They could end up in therapy regardless of how good or bad of a mom I was. And suddenly, like the mind-blown emoji popping up in a comic strip, I realized, *No, this is not the worst thing that could happen to them. Or to me.*

Thinking Styles

Eager to help me get to the root of my fear of being a bad mom, Janie introduced me to the Unhealthy Thinking Styles worksheet—a list of tendencies people fall into and the distortions they create.[20] We discussed each one and considered how it might be influencing my self-image. Take note of anything that jumps off the page for you as we go through them.

All-or-Nothing Thinking: Feeling like a failure if we don't do something perfectly. Categorizing things as black or white.

Mental Filter: Focusing only on the areas we've fallen short while giving no credit to our positive accomplishments.

Jumping to Conclusions: Imagining we know what another person is thinking. Attempting to read other peoples' minds or predict the future (also known as fortune telling).

Emotional Reasoning: Allowing our feelings to determine what is true. *(Since I feel embarrassed, I must be an idiot.)*

Labeling: Classifying ourselves and others based on our perceptions. *(I am utterly useless. He's such a moron. She's such a drama queen.)*

Over-generalizing: Drawing a broad conclusion or seeing a pattern based on a single event. *(Everything is always . . . Nothing is ever . . . You always . . . We never . . .)*

Disqualifying the Positive: Discounting something good that you have done.

Magnification (Catastrophizing)/Minimization: Making too big or too small an ordeal of something that has happened or could happen.

Critical Language (Should/Must): Criticizing ourselves and others with words like *should*, *must*, and *ought*.

Personalization: Heaping all the blame on yourself for something that was not your fault. Conversely, pointing the finger at someone else for something you did.

Any of those beliefs sound familiar, friend?

Browsing the page was like unlocking a stash of evidence from my secret mental mailbox. I saw proof of each of these unhelpful ways of thinking in my various relationships. I tended to label myself with friends and colleagues. With my husband, I jumped to conclusions and personalized. When it came to anything with my health or the safety of my kids, I catastrophized and went straight to worst-case scenarios. But as a mom, my go to mindset was all-or-nothing thinking.

As Janie and I surveyed the scene, it became clear I believed I was either doing everything right or everything wrong. I was either helping my kids or hurting them. There was no middle ground for grace. If I was doing well, I was acceptable, loveable, and worthy. But if I failed in any way, all the good was immediately discounted, and I became unacceptable, unlovable, and worthless. My kids were bound to end up in therapy because I was doomed to fail, regardless of how much time I invested in improving myself. No matter how hard I tried, it would never be enough, and I was too much of a mess not to mess up everything and everyone around me.

A Different Approach

Once Janie and I discerned that I was operating out of an all-or-nothing framework, she walked me through an exercise that continues to help me check in with my thinking and beliefs to this day. Let's look at an example together now.

At the top of the paper, I wrote down something bad I believed about myself. We then labeled it a lie, identified the fear that the lie was triggering, and acknowledged the behavior that resulted from that fear. At the bottom of the paper, we crafted a truth statement about how I was feeling, (re) framed the fear being triggered by the feeling, and acknowledged the behavior that resulted from (re)framing the fear.

Here's an example:

LIE:	FEAR:	RESULT:
I'm a bad mom.	My kids are going to end up in therapy because of me.	Freezes me in guilt and shame. Nowhere to go from here. Adds fuel to my belief that I'm a bad mom. If they need therapy, it must be because I failed as a mom.
TRUTH:	(RE)FRAME:	RESULT:
I notice that motherhood is challenging for me. Sometimes I have a hard time loving my kids well. My kids may end up in therapy for reasons other than my mistakes as a mom.	My kids ending up in therapy is not the worst thing that could happen—to them or to me. Everyone can benefit from the tools of therapy.	Acknowledges that just because something is hard doesn't mean I'm bad at it. Makes room for grace and growth.

Can you feel the freedom that comes from embracing a true statement about a hard reality?

Knowing that I would be part of my children's trauma made me feel like a failure, with a capital F. The fact that my pain would inevitably cause them pain did not scream *good mom* or even *good enough mom* to me. But considering that I could also be part of their healing did. Embracing the both/and of this scenario helped me see that God can restore things that have been torn down and renew things that have been devastated. Our failures can launch us forward toward healing and wholeness if we let them. Something that has helped me embrace this slow transformation is the concept of failing forward.

Failing Forward

Winston Churchill summed it up perfectly: "Success is not final, failure is not fatal: it is the courage to continue that counts."[21] To me, this is the epitome of failing forward. The first time I realized I had practiced it was, amazingly enough, after my mom-of-the year meltdown. In the heat of the moment, I had no idea that's what I had done. But looking back with the knowledge I now possess, I can see hope in the midst of one of my darkest moments.

After losing my ever-living mind with my kids, I fell to my knees, pulled my baby and toddler close to my heart, and apologized. I put words to how I was feeling, identified the specific actions and words that caused them pain, and then asked for their forgiveness. Identifying and explaining my feelings did not excuse my bad behavior, but it did help uncover the deeper work at play.

"Mommy is having a really hard time right now. I'm so sorry for yelling at you. I felt overwhelmed by how loud it was when you both were crying, and instead of taking a time-out and walking into the other room to catch my breath, I yelled at you, and that was not okay. I did not handle my feelings very well, and I'm so sorry for that. Would you please forgive me?"

My three-year-old's hazel green eyes looked so far into mine that for a moment I was sure she could see my soul.

"Yes, Mommy, I forgive you."

Failure is going to be something we experience over and over again. Pride, envy, bitterness, or anger will creep in, and before we know it, we're throwing temper tantrums, building walls, and burning bridges. All of us—our spouses, parents, coworkers, bosses, pastors, friends, kids, and selves—will know the sting of sin and the power it has to damage relationships. We're all going to say, do, think, and feel things we wish we hadn't. Romans 3:23 confirms it: "For all have sinned and fall short of the glory of God." But our shortcomings have the capacity to show us how the kindness of God leads us to repentance (Romans 2:4). And when failing forward, we will remind ourselves, and those we love, where to turn when we mess up: "If we confess our sins, he is faithful and just to forgive us our sins and to cleanse us from all unrighteousness" (1 John 1:9 ESV).

Kintsugi

We all have baggage and bad habits that can lead to brokenness in our faith, relationships, and self-worth. Sometimes, the very thing that breaks us is the tool God uses to shape us and show us His transformational love. He can make broken things beautiful again. I'll never forget the day Janie introduced me to *kintsugi*.

Kintsugi is the Japanese art of repairing broken pottery with precious metals. Instead of tossing the damaged pieces out, the artist uses the cracks of the restored ceramic to tell a story and showcase the beauty of the binding agent. Pure, priceless gold pulls pieces once torn apart from each other back together. And the vessel is truly more beautiful for having been broken.

This is what God does with us. He is the potter, and we are the clay. When we fall and break, he binds us back together with his perfect love. He makes beauty from our ashes. As I battle feeling like a bad mom, the art of kintsugi helps me remember that there is nothing broken that God cannot repair. This helps me accept the fact that if my kids end up in therapy because of my brokenness, they will also end up in therapy because of my healing.

As a family, we've all grown because of my time in therapy. At ages nine and eleven, my kids are more emotionally intelligent than I was at age thirty! I have learned a lot, but I'm still learning. I've healed a lot, but I'm still healing. I still have bad moments. But I know now that these bad moments do not make me a bad mom. They make me human. They make me ashes that God is turning into something more beautiful.

Whatever brokenness you are holding today, hear this: we serve a God who puts broken things back together. There is nothing unfixable for our mighty Maker. He repairs what is broken, restores what is devastated, and reconnects what is torn apart. What do you need to place in His skillful, healing hands today?

Now It's Your Turn

During my session with Janie, I was working through the fear that I was a bad mom. Your fear may relate to a challenging relationship with a spouse, parent, friend, or coworker. You may be doubting yourself because of your job, a past mistake, or a dream unfulfilled. Whether or not you have kids, I bet you can identify with the fear of messing up a relationship because of your insecurities and baggage. Deeper still, I imagine you understand the unbearable strain these unhelpful thinking patterns place on your sense of self-worth. Whatever it is, take a moment to think about the ways you label yourself.

Now write down some of the core beliefs you'd like to (re)frame. It may be helpful to work with a friend, coach, or counselor to come up with your truth statements. I once heard it said that we are the slowest to believe the truest thing about ourselves. How true this is. We need the eyes of others who see things in us that we don't yet see in ourselves.

LIE:	FEAR:	RESULT:
TRUTH:	(RE)FRAME:	RESULT:

Reclaiming Our Hope

The only all-or-nothing mindset we were ever meant to embrace is the absolute, never-ending, always faithful love of our Creator God. It is His deep, wide love that provides the foundation for renewing our minds and (re)framing our faith, identity, and mental health. It is His perfect love that grants us grace when we mess up and perseverance to fail forward. I love how Annie F. Downs describes this in her book *Looking for Lovely*:

> I have learned that to be all grace is to be lazy but to be all persever-ance is to be judgmental. A good balance of grace and perseverance pushes us forward without destroying our spirit when we don't meet a goal, and it continually brings us back to our goals, dreams, and desires in order to remember why we began, how far we've come to get here, and where we ultimately want to go. It gives us permission to not be perfect but to strive toward excellence.[22]

I'm never going to be a "perfect" mom, wife, woman, or leader. But I'm not altogether bad at these roles either. And neither are you.

I want to have a marriage that sets my children up for a lasting legacy in their own lives. I want to pursue meaningful ministry opportunities. And I want to not beat myself up when things don't go as I planned. I want to be intentional about noticing how far I've come, even though I have further to go in my healing. I want to strive toward excellence without suffocating in self-deprecation. Perhaps you want these things too?

Our God is willing and able to piece our broken hearts and frag-mented mindsets back together with His perfect love.

(RE)FRAME IT

Let's take a moment to identify how our beliefs affect our behavior, which lies need to be replaced with truth, and what steps we can take to move toward whole health.

WORLDVIEW: How has my upbringing affected my mindset?
Think back to the earliest time you can remember thinking an abso-lute truth about yourself, like "I always . . . I'll never . . . I'm such a . . ." Can you identify when this idea was planted in your mind? Is there a person, place, or experience tied to this memory?

BELIEFS: How has my worldview filtered what I believe to be true?

What experiences in your life helped this belief take root as truth?

VALUES: How have my beliefs framed what I value?

How have your beliefs about who you are framed where you put your energy and attention? Do you spend a lot of time worrying? Self-sabotaging? People pleasing? Trying to be perfect? Attempting to make up for lost time?

CHOICES: How have my values influenced my choices?

How have these values impacted your self-worth, relationships, and professional endeavors? Are you moving toward healthier habits, or are you stuck in a shame spiral?

RESULT: How have my choices helped or hurt me and those around me?

What would it look like to (re)frame that initial belief (I'm such a . . .) with a true statement about your hard reality? What step can you take today to move toward Jesus and into the light of His grace, forgiveness, and nourishment?

PRAY ABOUT IT

Elyashib, you are the God who restores. When the messiness of this world messes with my thinking, please bring these truths to mind: Your holy hands made me. I am loved by you. I am worthy because of you. I can face anything with your Spirit within me. And there is no mess, not even the ones I make, that can diminish my value, worth, or purpose. There is nothing broken that you can't bind and make more beautiful and more valuable than it was before.

When I'm tempted to believe absolute lies about myself, redirect my mind to your absolute truth. You know all my flaws and failures, yet you tirelessly pursue me with your love. When I'm tempted by the Enemy to doubt your goodness, remind me that I am connected to you. Help me not see my faults as absolute failures but as opportunities to grow. You can use my past mistakes to help me fail forward in my future mistakes.

Remind me that my kids ending up in therapy is not the worst thing that could happen. I may be part of their trauma, but I can choose to be actively involved in their healing. Help me see that you can use all of this. Every parenting blunder is a chance for me to show my children the power of repentance and the depth of your love no matter how many times I mess up. When I fail, I can fall into your arms where you pick me up, dust me off, and send me back into the game. Help me fail forward and live as an example of someone being changed by you.

In the name of the Father, the Son, and the Holy Spirit, amen.

MESSterpiece REMINDER:
With God's love and wisdom, I can fail forward and teach others to extend grace to themselves too.

Chapter 9

THE CRASHING WAVES OF CHRONIC ILLNESS

For I, the Lord, love justice; I hate robbery and wrongdoing. In my faithfulness I will reward my people and make an everlasting covenant with them. Their descendants will be known among the nations and their offspring among the peoples. All who see them will acknowledge that they are a people the Lord has blessed.

Isaiah 61:8–9

AS SHE STOOD AT THE shore of the ocean, watching the storm brewing in the distance, she dug her feet into the sand. The breeze that blew gently through her hair moments earlier became snappishly brisk against her back. Sprays that had tickled her toes soon splashed fiercely against her legs. With each glorious break, the water confirmed its intentions of unrelenting power.

She knew the storm was coming, but she couldn't move. There was no way out of this. She'd have to dig her feet in, bend her knees, and brace for an inevitable impact. The salty dew stung her cheeks. The brute force activated every muscle in her body. For a moment, she couldn't see or breathe or think. Her life flashed before her eyes, and she wondered if she'd make it out of this alive.

Suddenly, she was keenly aware of the sand between her toes. Through blurry droplets from the ocean deep, she watched the waves roll back into the sea, as all waves do. And she realized she was still standing. She had survived. She had welcomed the wave to come, she had stood her ground, and she had endured the storm.

As she patted her legs and pulled her hands up to her face to be sure she was, indeed, alive and intact, she felt simultaneously exhilarated and exhausted. The adrenaline of the event began to wear off, and her knees weakened beneath her. As her body began to give out, she found herself caught in the arms of someone strong and familiar. With all the strength she had left, she looked up.

"Daddy!" she gasped in deep relief. "You were here all along, weren't you?"

This was a visualization Janie had me do in one of our sessions to show me what it felt like to welcome the waves of anxiety and depression, while standing my ground against them. Perhaps you can see yourself in the mirage of this young woman too? Scared yet strong. Soaking wet yet still standing. Relieved to find she had not been alone yet amazed at her own resilience.

An Encounter with Abba

When I was standing on the proverbial shore, facing the overwhelming and unfamiliar waves of anxiety and depression, I had an experience where I could almost tangibly feel God's presence with me. Have you ever experienced that? Like you're in your body as it is now, but you can see yourself outside of time for a moment? Kind of like Scrooge in *A Christmas Carol* as he peers in through the window of his life. I know it sounds strange, but hang with me.

I saw myself as a five-year-old little girl sitting on the floor, knees pulled up under my chin, and tears streaming down my face. God appeared just like a normal dad in a T-shirt, jeans, and slippers. He sat on the couch and lifted me up onto His lap. Holding me close, we had an honest conversation about the road ahead.

His words were sincere but not sugar-coated. He said things would get worse before they got better and harder before they got easier. My healing would actually require me to endure more pain for a season before I would see any fruit from the hard work I was about to begin. The five-year-old in me protested, "But I don't wanna!"

He smiled and promised me two things: He would be with me, and He would use my story to bring hope to others who were also hurting. He reminded me that I wasn't the first one of His children to come through desperate circumstances. I found myself in solidarity with my ancestors as I recalled the story of the descendants of Abraham in the book of Isaiah. The Israelites endured pain, slavery, oppression, and feelings of abandonment. So had I. They had questioned God's goodness and doubted He would truly set them free. So had I. Yet time and again, God remained faithful to His promises. The same thing He told His children centuries before held true for me too:

> Don't be afraid, for I am with you. Don't be discouraged, for
> I am your God. I will strengthen you and help you. I will hold
> you up with my victorious right hand. (Isaiah 41:10 NLT)

This encouragement from God's Word took on new meaning that day. And I can say to you now, several years later, He was true to His word. He kept both promises. He has been with me. He has strengthened me. He has helped me. And He has used my story to bring hope and healing to others.

You're holding this book in your hands because He held my hands. And He will hold your hands too. He taught me how to stand firm in my faith when life shook me to my core. He can do the same for you. He taught me how to ask for help and lean into the divinely crafted giftings of those He designed to be doctors, nurses, scientists, therapists, counselors, coaches, and pastors. He can do the same for you. He gave me fresh eyes to see Him as the Creator, who wove together every intricate function of our bodies, each designed to fulfill a unique plan and purpose throughout our lives—not only for our benefit but for the benefit of others. He can do the same for you.

In my story, and maybe in yours too, God did not snap His fingers and cure my diseases. Instead, He showed up and showed off His mighty mercy through the storms of my life. In the middle of the mess. Not once the mess was cleaned up, but in my mess and with my mess. His presence with me through it all has helped me (re)frame my place and purpose in this world. I am a *messterpiece*. And God can use all my brokenness to showcase His beautiful, binding love to hurting people. He can do the same for you.

A Moment at the Manger

I don't know what time of year it is as you read this, but allow me a moment to take us into the season of Advent and talk about the birth of Jesus. His origin story is, after all, relevant whether or not it's December. The circumstances He faced during His life offer encouragement and wisdom for us as we find ourselves in similar situations. His life proves that doing the will of the Father is not always easy, but it's always worth it.

Reading back through the Gospel of Luke reminds me how complex it is to be human, even if you are God Himself. Things got messy the moment an angel appeared to a teenage girl with news that she was the one God had chosen to bring His Son into the world. You'd think someone who was highly favored and chosen by God would have a life filled with comfort, ease, and prosperity. But Mary, Joseph, and Jesus led lives that were anything but comfortable, easy, and prosperous. They met adversity from the moment they said yes to God. They faced trials and tribulations every step of the way. If this is what life looks like for God's chosen people, what hope is there for the rest of us?

Lots.

The thing about God's favor is that it's not about comfort; it's about change. It's not about making things easy; it's about making them possible. It's not about health and wealth, it's about heaven coming down to earth to bridge a gap that was too wide to bear. The Father loves us so much that He sent His Son. Jesus loves us so much that He humbled Himself to enter human history as a baby born in a stable, only to grow into a man who would die on a cross. The Holy Spirit loves us so much that He chooses to reside within us, giving us strength and help until we are reunited with our Creator face to face.

Jesus's coming had been foretold by the prophets for hundreds of years. The people plagued by oppression had been waiting generations for the Messiah to arrive. And then, one ordinary night, a blinding light appeared in the sky, and history as we know it was changed forever. We can relate to the people of Israel who eagerly waited for the Savior to come and make everything better. But Jesus didn't do things the way anyone expected. He didn't appear as a warrior and immediately overthrow the corrupt government. He came as a lowly servant to walk the dusty roads beside us, to be persecuted with us, and then to be sacrificed for us. This was how He chose to show us the full extent of His love. And He invites us to follow Him and live by His example.

An Invitation

Saying yes to God does not take away our pain and problems. It doesn't eliminate disease and death. But it does bring heaven near—welcoming the supernatural into the ordinary and inviting hope into our hearts, both for the here and now and for the soon but not yet. Loving Jesus doesn't guarantee comfort, ease, and prosperity, but it does promise faith, hope, and love (1 Corinthians 13:13).

The waves of anxiety, depression, and chronic illness are big, scary, and erratic. Blue skies can transform into storm clouds in the blink of an eye, bringing with them big currents that are hard to withstand. The fear of the waves can easily overtake us. It can rattle our faith and make us weak in the knees. But mixed into those waves is God's peace, kindness, and grace. Infused in the water of that ocean is living hope that is unable to be drowned by fear. He will be with us. He will strengthen us. He will help us. He will hold us up. He will never let us go.

As I think back to the illustration Janie gave me in our first session, the lyrics of the popular worship song "Oceans: Where Feet May Fail," by Hillsong United, swirl around in my head and heart. The stanzas are a prayer, asking the Spirit of God to lead us into unbounded trust in His presence as He calls us out into the mysterious unknown—a space that will likely be uncomfortable, painful, and filled with adversity. Oh, how I want that kind of trust in God. How desperately I want my faith to withstand the storms of this life. And as I look down at my own feet in the sand when wave after wave crashes over me, I realize I am never alone. Jesus really is with me in the storm. Even when I doubt Him, He never lets go.

He'll never let you go either.

(RE)FRAME IT

Let's take a moment to identify how our beliefs affect our behavior, which lies need to be replaced with truth, and what steps we can take to move toward whole health.

WORLDVIEW: How has my upbringing affected my mindset?
Was the concept of hearing from God, or feeling like God was speaking to you, commonly talked about in your home growing up? (Not as an audible voice but in a way you understood was Him.)

BELIEFS: How has my worldview filtered what I believe to be true?
If you have heard God speak to you, what was that like for you? How would you describe hearing from God to someone else?

VALUES: How have my beliefs framed what I value?
If you've shared those experiences with others, did they understand and express having had similar experiences? Or did they look at you sideways, unsure of how to grasp what you were talking about?

CHOICES: How have my values influenced my choices?
When you heard from God or felt an inclination that He was pointing you in a certain direction, or away from it, how did you respond?

RESULT: How have my choices helped or hurt me and those around me?
Is there anything you feel God is saying to you today?

PRAY ABOUT IT

Emmanuel, you are the God who is with us. Remind me that you are still my hope. Even when I'm hurting. Even when things are hard. Even when I can't see the light at the end of the tunnel. When I don't understand what you're doing, help me to trust that you can see the beginning and the end and that you have my ultimate good in mind—even though I may have to go through the valley on the way.

Lord, thank you for always loving me and never leaving me. Thank you for not avoiding my mess but getting down into the depths of the dirt with me. Thank you for reminding me of who I am and helping me let go of who I am not.

You are still the one I can put my faith and hope in. Your love breaks through the pain of this world and helps me persevere. Your love breaks through the power of sin and offers me reconciliation and salvation. Your love is what makes hope and faith possible.

Thank you for humbling yourself and coming as a baby. Thank you for the suffering you endured with me in mind. Thank you for bringing light into the darkness.

In the name of the Father, the Son, and the Holy Spirit, amen.

MESSterpiece REMINDER:

Even though the waves will crash over me, they will not take me down because God has promised to be with me through the storm.

Chapter 10

DON'T DESPISE SMALL BEGINNINGS

For as the soil makes the sprout come up and a garden causes seeds to grow, so the Sovereign Lord will make righteousness and praise spring up before all nations.

Isaiah 61:11

DID YOU KNOW A FULL-GROWN oak tree can take twenty to thirty years to produce its first acorn?[23] #mindblown

Walking through Marshalls one afternoon, a small wooden sign caught my eye. Painted on a pale pink background, the words arched above an open hand holding a single seed: "Bloom in grace, grow in love." The seed had sprouted a tiny shoot with four little leaves. And I just stared at it, almost as if looking in a mirror, contemplating the seeds inside of me.

This little gem now sits on the corner of my writing desk, where I'm sitting now, pondering the beauty and complexity of small beginnings. Compared to the flurry of leaves on a fully grown oak tree, the foliage in my painting seems minuscule. But when we remember that every towering oak tree in the world was birthed from a tiny little seed, just like this one, our perspective widens, and hope rises up to meet us.

You and I are like tiny seeds, bursting with glorious potential. But we don't mature into oaks of righteousness overnight (Isaiah 61:4). You don't get shade from a tree's branches the day it's planted. Little by little, year after year, seeds absorb the nutrients from the soil, their roots grow deeper, their trunk grows stronger, and eventually, it begins to produce fruit that brings beauty and nourishment to the world around it. In the waiting, we must remember all that's happening under the surface—out of sight but not out of mind.

Seeds

"Isn't it funny how day by day nothing changes, but when you look back, everything is different?" This popular quote, commonly credited to C.S. Lewis, perfectly describes the process of growth, change, and (re) framing. Day by day, the fruit of our labor doesn't seem to add up to much. But after a while, we realize we are not the same. Things really have begun to shift in our mindsets. Our faith is stronger. Our identity is more intact. Our capacity to love and be loved has increased.

There is hope hidden in the hardship that things will work out no matter how difficult things get for a season. When we come out on the other side of tribulation, we want others to know it's possible for them too. That's why and how you're holding this book in your hands. I pray that as you've journeyed with me through some dark nights and stormy days, you have felt seen, heard, known, and supported.

Learning to be tended by the Gardener of our body, mind, and soul will be a lifelong journey. Trauma and dysfunction stunt our growth, arrest our emotional development, and convince us we're too far gone and incapable of change. But in the garden of our Creator's love, we can begin to produce the good and life-giving fruit of love, joy, peace, patience, kindness, goodness, faithfulness, gentleness, and self-control (Galatians 5:22–23). Attached to the vine of Jesus's life-giving presence, we tap into the grit and guidance required to dig up lies rooted in shame, fear, and pain and reestablish the seeds of our identity in the soil of His truth.

The Renewal of Our Minds

Trees begin as a seed and renewal begins as a thought. In order to be transformed from a malnourished sapling into an oak of righteousness, we must allow God to renew our minds. It is in our minds that we have formed unhealthy thought patterns that have shaped unhealthy behavior patterns. Thankfully, our Creator God designed us with the mind-blowing capacity to, quite literally, be transformed from the inside out. And it all begins in our minds (Romans 12:2).

Replacing old habits and neural pathways with new ones requires the hard, sweaty, uncomfortable work of digging deep into the dirt (our worldview), uprooting what's diseased (our unhealthy thoughts, feelings, and actions), and replenishing the earth with healthy soil where you can plant a brand-new tree (our healthy thoughts, feelings, and actions). Just like starting a garden, a new health program, or a big project, it will take time to see the sprouts of growth from the seeds we've planted.

As you've discovered throughout this book, change did not come quickly for me. The roots of my unhealthy beliefs and behaviors ran deep. I had a lot of digging up and replanting to do. It took a year of meeting with my therapist once a week, *plus* a twelve-week topical class through my hospital called RSR (Rapid Symptom Reduction), *plus* a nine-month behavior and relationship education program called Life Skills International, *plus* beginning medication for my anxiety and depression before I began to notice shifts in my thinking, changes in my behavior, and freedom in my faith. And I will ever be tending the garden of my mind. It's not a once-and-done event. 'Cuz, you know, weeds.

Even though this is the last chapter of the book, I pray it's not the last time you'll pick this book up. I've put together some tangible tools that continue to help me tend the garden of my mind, body, and soul, and I hope they're helpful for you too. Please pardon the cheesy title of the section, but I can't resist a good alliteration.

In hopes of guiding you into further exploration of (re)framing your mindset and expanding your capacity to remain in Jesus's love, I give you Seven Ways to Start Small. (I told you it was cheesy, but I promise it's a meaty plan. See what I did there?)

Okay, here we go.

Seven Ways to Start Small

- Seek Support
- Search Scripture

- Speak Kindly to Yourself
- Set Up a Bedtime Routine
- Start Tapping
- Study Your Strengths
- Starve the Lies

SEEK SUPPORT

"The Christian life isn't just difficult to do alone, it's impossible."[24] The former lead pastor at our church, Steve Clifford, often reminded us of this truth. We were never meant to do life alone: not during the bad times or the good. Though community and counsel require vulnerability, it is one of our greatest assets in discovering the depth of God's love for us. Seeking the support of a friend, pastor, counselor, coach, or therapist is a crucial component of healthy growth.

For me, this began in my MOPS group—around a table. In my fear, I took a vulnerable step to let myself be known. Instead of the rejection I feared, I was met with open arms and realized I was not the only one who felt insecure and intimidated. These women are now my people. And every time I allow myself to be vulnerable and let the real me shine through—in all of its brokenness—I find more of my people. It's what gave me the courage to seek out professional therapy, become more assertive with my doctors, and show up in group settings where I didn't know a soul.

Consider a community or support system you can bravely seek out today.

SEARCH SCRIPTURE

The Word of God is the source of absolute truth. Knowing what the Bible actually says about who we are to God and who God is to us is our strongest weapon against the lies that threaten our physical, spiritual, emotional, and mental health. But don't let logistics get in the way of finding a rhythm that works for you. There's no set amount of time you have to read your Bible every day to be a *good Christian*. And reading the Bible certainly doesn't magically make all your problems disappear. But take it from me, the less time we spend in Scripture, the more time the Enemy has to fill our minds with lies. Searching the Scriptures to see what God says is how we weed out lies and water truth.

What God has to say about you and me in His Word is truly magnificent. He loves us so much. He fights for us and is truly near to the brokenhearted. I've partnered truth statements with Scripture to help solidify these realities in our hearts and minds. Say these out loud as you read and anytime you need to remember who you are and whose you are.

I was made on purpose for a purpose.

"Long before he laid down earth's foundations, he had us in mind, had settled on us as the focus of his love, to be made whole and holy by his love. Long, long ago he decided to adopt us into his family through Jesus Christ. (What pleasure he took in planning this!) He wanted us to enter into the celebration of his lavish gift-giving by the hand of his beloved Son." (Ephesians 1:4 MSG)

"For we are God's masterpiece. He has created us anew in Christ Jesus, so we can do the good things he planned for us long ago." (Ephesians 2:10 NLT)

"You have been chosen by God Himself—you are priests of the King, you are holy and pure, you are God's very own—all this so that you may show to others how God called you out of the darkness into his wonderful light." (1 Peter 2:9 TLB)

I am unconditionally loved.

"Can anything ever separate us from Christ's love? Does it mean he no longer loves us if we have trouble or calamity, or are persecuted, or hungry, or destitute, or in danger, or threatened with death? . . . No, despite all these things, overwhelming victory is ours through Christ, who loved us. And I am convinced that nothing can ever separate us from God's love. Neither death nor life, neither angels nor demons, neither our fears for today nor our worries about tomorrow—not even the powers of hell can separate us from God's love. No power in the sky above or in the earth below—indeed, nothing in all creation will ever be able to separate us from the love of God that is revealed in Christ Jesus our Lord." (Romans 8:35–39 NLT)

I am valuable.

"For you know that God paid a ransom to save you from the empty life you inherited from your ancestors. And it was not paid with mere gold or silver, which lose their value. It was the precious blood of Christ, the sinless, spotless Lamb of God." (1 Peter 1:18–19 NLT)

I am protected.

"But now, O Jacob, listen to the LORD who created you. O Israel, the one who formed you says, 'Do not be afraid, for I have ransomed you. I have called you by name; you are mine. When you go through deep waters, I will be with you. When you go through rivers of difficulty, you will not drown. When you walk through the fire of oppression, you will not be burned up; the flames will not consume you. For I am the LORD, your God, the Holy One of Israel, your Savior.'" (Isaiah 43:1–3 NLT)

"But I am like a sheltered olive tree protected by the Lord himself. I trust in the mercy of God forever and ever." (Psalm 52:8 TLB)

SPEAK TO YOURSELF KINDLY

One of the first things we did in the Life Skills course was work through our self-talk scripts. Each day we were tasked with standing in front of the mirror and speaking a list of positive affirmations out loud to ourselves. Yep, it was pretty awkward. But I was ready for change.

I taped the list to my bathroom mirror so I was sure to see it. I recorded myself speaking into my phone, and I'd listen to the voice memos on my morning walks. It all felt very strange, and I was skeptical. But, to my surprise, after a month of clumsily working out my mind muscles, I noticed a distinct difference in how I felt. What once seemed ridiculous now seemed reasonable. Statements I had never been able to use before to describe myself now felt comfortable on my lips.

It was like trying on a pair of jeans I was sure would be too small, but instead of struggling to pull them over my hips, the zipper went up smoothly and the button looped through without any muffin top. You know what I'm talking about! And you know nothing beats that feeling. It's the same when we unlearn negative beliefs and replace them with truth.

Here are a few of the statements I practiced believing:

- I am valuable.
- I can have a healthy self-image.
- I accept myself the way I am.
- I love myself the way I am.
- I can ask for what I need assertively while still being respectful.
- I can set specific goals for my future and work enthusiastically to achieve them.
- I am learning new ways to express my feelings appropriately.
- I cannot control what happens, but I'm learning to control my attitude no matter my circumstance.
- I can forgive those who have wronged me.

These are just a handful of statements I used. Today, I encourage you to borrow these and begin rewriting the script in your mind. What we believe impacts how we behave, but we don't have to keep believing lies. Try these truth statements on for size for yourself and see how practicing them changes how you feel.

(There's also a fantastic list of affirmations in the Mistaken Beliefs chapter of the *Anxiety and Phobia Workbook*[25]).

SET UP A BEDTIME ROUTINE

This one may seem out of place, but I promise you it's one of the best investments of time you'll ever make. Research shows that going to bed and waking up at the same time every day can do wonders for your mood and mental health. A tired mind and body are not up to the task of battling lies with truth. The wearier we are, the weaker our defenses become, and our risk of giving in to temptation skyrockets.

Keep a journal by your bed to document how you feel so you can pick up on patterns. The idea is to get your body into a rhythm that's relaxing. You may take a hot bath, do some light stretching, read a chapter of a book, write down three things you're thankful for, or spend time in prayer or meditation.

Take the time to figure out how many hours of sleep your body needs and make it a priority to set up and stick to a bedtime routine. If you need to wake up at 6:00 a.m., and you know your body needs eight hours of sleep to feel rested, then make it a priority to be in bed by 10:00 p.m. Sure, you may sacrifice catching that episode of your favorite show, but it won't take long to see it was a sacrifice well made.

START TAPPING

Tapping, also known as EFT or emotional freedom techniques, combines modern psychology with ancient Chinese acupressure, and it has done wonders for me. By tapping on certain meridian points of our body, a calming signal is sent to the amygdala of our brain, where our fight, flight, and freeze response is triggered. Once our brain registers that it is safe, it can begin to relax. As our body relaxes, we can tune in to what we are feeling emotionally, which helps us manage how we are feeling physically. EFT can provide relief from a variety of ailments, including chronic illness, PTSD, anxiety, depression, and phobias.[26] Many therapists are familiar with EFT and can incorporate it into their sessions.

I recommend downloading The Tapping Solution App on your smartphone.

https://www.thetappingsolution.com/

Psychologists and siblings Nick and Jessica Ortner offer hundreds of guided sessions on topics ranging from anxiety, anger, and depression support, to forgiveness, self-worth, and motivation to work, finish a project, and make healthier food choices. They even have sessions designed for kids! Most sessions are less than fifteen minutes, and some are micro boosts at less than five minutes, and they are incredibly effective. You can try the app for free for two weeks, listening to as many sessions as you like, and then it's $95 for an annual subscription. I can honestly say it's one of the best hundred bucks I've ever spent.

A few of my favorite sessions are:

- Releasing Anxiety (Emotional Freedom)

- Instant Boost of Gratitude (great for car rides to and from school or work)
- Micro Boost of Muscle Tension Relief
- Support Your Healing: Thyroid Problems (Louise Hay Collection)
- Jaw Relaxation Sleep Programming
- Calming the Body and Mind for Sleep (for kids)

STUDY YOUR STRENGTHS

God has divinely designed each of us with specific personalities and gift sets that bring something useful into the world. Understanding how we're wired opens up valuable insight into our relationships, careers, and interests. If you're like me and don't like to be boxed into a type—fear not. The goal of studying our strengths is to discover where we excel so we can more confidently step into those roles and settings.

Here's a list of assessments that have helped me over the years:

Understanding Your Temperament

https://www.betterhelp.com/advice/temperament/4-most-common-temperament-types/

Clifton Strength Finders Assessment and Coaching

https://www.gallup.com/cliftonstrengths/

Myers Briggs Personality Test

https://www.themyersbriggs.com/

DISC Personality Assessment

https://internalchange.com/what-is-disc/

LOGR (The Four Animals Personality Test)

https://www.focusonthefamily.com/marriage/4-animals-personality-test/

Enneagram

https://www.enneagraminstitute.com/how-the-enneagram-system-works

Spiritual Gifts Assessment

https://www.lifeway.com/en/articles/women-leadership-spiritual-gifts-growth-service

STARVE THE LIES

Remember those old Special K commercials that asked, "What will you gain when you lose?" When people stepped onto the scale, instead of seeing a number, they were shocked to see words like confidence, joy, and freedom. Their whole demeanor changed with a simple (re)frame of their health journey: "What could I gain if I lost?"

When we lose the weight of fear, shame, and guilt, we gain the capacity for confidence, joy, and freedom. A healthy garden can only grow once the weeds have been pulled. And they have to be pulled again and again. Weeds have to be pulled, lies have to be starved, and truth has to be tended.

We are slow to believe things that are true about who we are yet destructively quick to root our identity in falsehoods, misrepresentations, and fabrications. Isn't this maddening? The further rooted our beliefs, the stronger they become—good and bad. So we literally must starve the lies that tell us we're too much and not enough and start embracing our divine design, even before we've fully arrived.

Slow Growth Is Still Growth

Let's be honest—growth is hard, pruning is painful, and old habits die hard.

Our spirits struggle to walk the narrow path to peace when the fields of fury lay wide open. Even when we make huge strides in growth and maturity, there will always be a need for nourishment, pruning, plowing, and planting. I find myself in this tricky space of having learned a lot during my road to healing yet feeling like I still know nothing at all. I'm telling others about the hope and solidarity available to them, yet I still battle anxious nights and dark days. My instinct is to believe I have nothing to say, even though God Himself told me to speak. My inclination is to feel stuck by anxiety and depression, even though I now have tools to help me live with them. The both/and of life is so unnerving sometimes—vastly complex yet soberingly simple.

But the fact remains that every ounce of energy, time, and intentionality we put toward healing, embracing a healthy mindset, and learning to remain in Jesus's love equals an ounce of growth. And small growth is still growth. When we're in the beginning phases of this lifelong journey, much of our development is happening under the surface—a tiny seed learning to let its roots grow down into new, nutritious soil. It's easy to forget what's happening under the surface when the growth above the soil seems to be taking forever. It's easy to get discouraged and feel like we're failing to make progress, but I like how Robert Orben reframes this: "Don't think of it as failure. Think of it as time-released success."[27]

Don't despise these small beginnings, friend. They are sprouting seeds of a glorious garden within you and within me.

(RE)FRAME IT

Let's take a moment to identify how our beliefs affect our behavior, which lies need to be replaced with truth, and what steps we can take to move toward whole health.

WORLDVIEW: How has my upbringing affected my mindset?
Name the lie you most believe to be true about yourself.

BELIEFS: How has my worldview filtered what I believe to be true?
Which truth from Scripture will help you starve that lie?

VALUES: How have my beliefs framed what I value?
Which of the I am/I can statements most resonated with you? Choose one to repeat to yourself every day this week.

CHOICES: How have my values influenced my choices?
Who is a trusted voice of truth in your life that you can reach out to for support?

RESULT: How have my choices helped or hurt me and those around me?
As you take your next step, remember to (re)frame:

- **R**emember who you are and whose you are
- **E**ducate yourself on your illnesses and your options
- **F**ind a friend, coach, pastor, counselor, or therapist to talk to and journey with
- **R**elease unforgiveness
- **A**djust your mindset
- **M**ake peace with making mistakes
- **E**mbrace Jesus and His unshakable love for you

PRAY ABOUT IT

I can think of no better way to end our time than to echo the prayer of Paul in Ephesians 3:14–21 (NLT):

> When I think of all this, I fall to my knees and pray to the Father, the Creator of everything in heaven and on earth. I pray that from his glorious, unlimited resources he will empower you with inner strength through his Spirit. Then Christ will make his home in your hearts as you trust in him. Your roots will grow down into God's love and keep you strong. And may you have the power to understand, as all God's people should, how wide, how long, how high, and how deep his love is. May you experience the love of Christ, though it is too great to understand fully. Then you will be made complete with all the fullness of life and power that comes from God. Now all glory to God, who is able, through his mighty power at work within us, to accomplish infinitely more than we might ask or think. Glory to him in the church and in Christ Jesus through all generations forever and ever! Amen.

MESSterpiece REMINDER:
Life is not without suffering, but suffering is not without hope. It's both/ and. And so am I.

FINAL THOUGHTS: THE END IS THE BEGINNING

A BOOK IS NEVER FINISHED. It just gets printed at the point the author feels they have done the best they can with the message they hope to convey. Putting printed words out into the world is a strange feeling. You know some will resonate with your story, and others won't. Some will recommend it to a friend, while others will leave a one-star review on Amazon. Many will find hope and strength to take their next step, while others will find they have so much more work ahead of them.

A person is never finished either. Until Jesus returns and all things are made new, we will continually be learning, changing, growing, and failing forward. As this book goes out into the world, I am practicing the art of grace for myself and for every person who reads this book. I have been as attuned to the Spirit of God as I possibly could be as I've worked on this project for the past several years. I have prayed, wept, studied, researched, contemplated, sought wise counsel, and made investments in my professional and spiritual development in order to offer hope and solidarity to those who are hurting. Keeping Scripture in context has been my greatest goal, but I'm sure someone somewhere will find fault in how I've used it, and I can only ask for your grace and your gentle feedback.

Throughout this journey, I've faced health challenges that added months to my timeline. Many times, I wondered if I'd ever actually finish the task God had entrusted to me. With only a couple of chapters left to finish my first draft, I got stuck—my words lodged between that notorious rock and hard place. Something was holding me back, but I didn't know what. I was reading *Looking for Lovely* by Annie F. Downs at the time and was profoundly comforted to learn that she, too, hit a dry spell during her writing process. In a conversation with a friend, she shared feeling like something was missing from the manuscript, but she couldn't quite put her finger on what it was. The words of wisdom he spoke to her felt like they were written just for me: "You know that just to finish the book doesn't require you to be a finished product, right?"[28]

The tears I didn't know were just under the surface spilled out of my soul. I sat stunned for several minutes. That was it! I'd unknowingly convinced myself that releasing this book into the world meant I needed to be a perfect representation of the hope and healing I wrote about. *Hello, distorted thinking, my old friend.* I was afraid that since I clearly had more work to do in my own healing journey that I was unfit to offer myself as any sort of authority on the subject. But that would be 100 percent incorrect.

My mess does not disqualify my masterpiece. My offerings do not need to be perfect to be meaningful. My need for further healing does not disqualify me from sharing what God has already done in my life. The same is true for you, dear friend.

As you take steps to shatter stigmas and (re)frame your fears, I pray you will continue to find yourself fully loved as the divinely crafted, beloved, and chosen daughter of the Master Artist and Creator. You may feel like a mess, but you are forever His masterpiece.

QUICK REFERENCE RESOURCE GUIDE

Visit my website for links to helpful resources for mental, physical, spiritual, and emotional health at www.AndreaMNyberg.com/Resources

Organizations

Find a therapist in your area or online at https://www.betterhelp.com/

Find a Life Skills International class near you at https://www.lifeskillsintl.org/

Find support with NAMI (National Alliance on Mental Illness) at https://nami.org

Books & Courses

The Anxiety and Phobia Workbook by Edmund J. Bourne, PhD

The Exchange Course (Includes Workbook & Teaching Videos) by Karrie Garcia

Freedom Academy (trauma-informed education) https://www.karrie-garcia.com/freedomacademy

About the Author

Andrea is an author, speaker, and photographer passionate about (re) framing fear and finding freedom in the middle of the mess. She holds a master of arts in educational leadership from Gateway Seminary and has maintained a faithful, referral-driven clientele in her photography business since 2012. A previous leader at her local MOPS (Mothers of Preschoolers) group, Andrea now enjoys speaking to groups across the San Francisco Bay Area.

These days, Andrea carpools kids around town, sings on the worship team at her church, and fails to keep her house from getting cluttered on a regular basis. Her southern accent sneaks out every once in a while, and her boisterous laugh can be heard from miles away. She is quick to encourage but slow to empty the dishwasher.

Andrea lives in San Jose, California, with her husband and two children.

Connect with Andrea on Instagram and Facebook @AndreaMNyberg and sign up for her newsletter at www.AndreaMNyberg.com.

ENDNOTES

1. "The Belief Tree," Darlene Cunningham with David Joel Hamilton and Dawn Gauslin, 2014, https://ywam.org/for-ywamers/the-belief-tree.

2. "The Moral Poverty of the West: Its Cause, Effects, and Solution," Darrow Miller with Gary Brumbelow, October 13, 2011, http://darrowmillerandfriends.com/2011/10/13/the-moral-poverty-of-the-west-its-cause-effects-and-solution/.

3. Darlene Cunningham, with Dawn Gauslin and Sean Lambert, *Values Matter: Stories of the Beliefs & Values that Shaped Youth With A Mission* (Seattle: YWAM Publishing, 2020).

4. "Slideshow: Anxiety Risk Factors," WebMD, 2019, https://www.facebook.com/WebMD, https://www.webmd.com/anxiety-panic/ss/slideshow-anxiety-risk-factors.

5. Edmund J Bourne, *The Anxiety and Phobia Workbook*, 7th Edition (Oakland: New Harbinger Publications Inc., 2020), 47.

6. Jeanie Lerche Davis, "What Are Anxiety Disorders?," WebMD, June 25, 2020, https://www.webmd.com/anxiety-panic/guide/anxiety-disorders.

7. "Panic Attacks and Panic Disorder—Symptoms and Causes," Mayo Clinic, May 4, 2018, https://www.mayoclinic.org/diseases-conditions/panic-attacks/symptoms-causes/syc-20376021.

8. "Depression (Major Depressive Disorder)," Mayo Clinic, February 3, 2018, https://www.mayoclinic.org/diseases-conditions/depression/symptoms-causes/syc-20356007.

9. "Depression (Major Depressive Disorder)," Mayo Clinic, February 3, 2018, https://www.mayoclinic.org/diseases-conditions/depression/symptoms-causes/syc-20356007.

10. *Merriam-Webster*, s.v. "regret," accessed December 13, 2022, https://www.merriam-webster.com/dictionary/regret.

11. *Merriam-Webster*, s.v. "remorse," accessed December 13, 2022, https://www.merriam-webster.com/dictionary/remorse.

12.   Lysa TerKeurst, *Forgiving What You Can't Forget: Discover How to Move On, Make Peace with Painful Memories, and Create a Life That's Beautiful Again* (Nashville: Nelson Books, 2020), 45–47.

13.   Paul Hegstrom, *Broken Children, Grown-up Pain: Understanding the Effects of Your Wounded Past* (Kansas City: Beacon Hill Press of Kansas City, 2006), 25.

14.   Bessel Van Der Kolk, *The Body Keeps the Score: Mind, Brain and Body in the Transformation of Trauma* (London: Penguin Books, 2014), 96–100.

15.   "Building Relationships Across Cultures: Are You a Peach or a Coconut?" Cultural Mixology, 2020, https://culturalmixology.com/relationship-building-are-you-a-peach-or-a-coconut/.

16.   Lysa TerKeurst, "The Rejection Infection," LysaTerKeurst.com, October 7, 2016, https://lysaterkeurst.com/2016/10/07/the-rejection-infection/.

17.   Brené Brown, *The Gifts of Imperfection* (Center City, MN: Hazelden Publishing, 2010), 39.

18.   Brown, *The Gifts of Imperfection*, 40.

19.   Timothy and Kathy Keller, *The Meaning of Marriage* (New York: Penguin Books, 2016).

20.   "Unhelpful Thinking Styles—Psychology Tools," Psychology Tools, 2018, https://www.psychologytools.com/resource/unhelpful-thinking-styles/.

21.   https://www.brainyquote.com/authors/winston-churchill-quotes.

22.   Annie F. Downs, *Looking for Lovely: Collecting the Moments That Matter* (Nashville: Lifeway Christian Resources, 2016), 167.

23.   "How Long Does It Take for a Tree to Grow?" Local Tree Estimates, accessed August 17, 2022, https://localtreeestimates.com/how-long-does-it-take-for-a-tree-to-grow/.

24.   Steve Clifford, WestGate Church.

25. Edmund J. Bourne, *Anxiety and Phobia Workbook, 7th ed.* (Oakland, CA: New Harbinger Publications, 2020).

26. "Tapping 101—Learn the Basics of the Tapping Technique," The Tapping Solution, www.thetappingsolution.com, accessed August 17, 2022, https://www.thetappingsolution.com/tapping-101/.

27. Robert Orben Quotes, BrainyQuote.com, accessed December 13, 2022, https://www.brainyquote.com/quotes/robert_orben_121334.

28. Annie F. Downs, *Looking for Lovely* (Nashville: B&H Books, 2016), 177–8.

ORDER INFORMATION

REDEMPTION
P R E S S

To order additional copies of this book, please visit
www.redemption-press.com.
Also available at Amazon, Christian bookstores,
and Barnes and Noble.

CPSIA information can be obtained
at www.ICGtesting.com
Printed in the USA
BVHW091104060423
661866BV00005B/788